SA'DI *in* LOVE

'Homa Katouzian's sympathetic and approachable translations of a selection of more than seventy of Sa'di's ghazals (short lyric poems) will introduce one of Iran's most significant poets to a new range of readers. Sa'di was a contemporary of Rumi and the most significant Shirazi poet of his time. In order to understand Persian poetry better, we surely must acquaint ourselves with Sa'di's lyrical genius.'

Dominic Parviz Brookshaw, Associate Professor of Persian Literature, University of Oxford

'In this volume of love, wine, handsome cupbearers, roses and nightingales Dr Katouzian opens the door to one of the treasures of Persian culture, the poetry of Sa'di, a champion of towering figures such as Sir William Jones, Ralph Waldo Emerson, and Voltaire. In this fascinating bilingual collection of love songs, Dr Katouzian's learned introduction and the beautiful and musical English translation capture the true spirit and sentiments of Persian culture, rendering the subtleties of the psychology of love, both spiritual and profane. This collection is a superb example of Persian poetry, showing why classical Persian poets are living heroes in Persian cultural areas, venerated in Iran, Afghanistan, Tajikistan and Central Asia.'

Ali-Asghar Seyed-Ghorab, Associate Professor of Persian, Leiden University

HOMA KATOUZIAN is a historian and literary critic, with a special interest in Iranian studies. He is the Iran Heritage Research Fellow at St Antony's College, Oxford. He is also the editor of *Iranian Studies*, the bimonthly journal of the International Society for Iranian Studies.

Sa'di in Love

The Lyrical Verses of Persia's Master Poet

HOMA KATOUZIAN

ILLUSTRATED BY MAHBOBE GHODS

I.B. TAURIS
LONDON • NEW YORK • OXFORD • NEW DELHI • SYDNEY

Published in association with the Roshan Cultural Institute

I.B. TAURIS
Bloomsbury Publishing Plc
50 Bedford Square, London, WC1B 3DP, UK
1385 Broadway, New York, NY 10018, USA
29 Earlsfort Terrace, Dublin 2, Ireland

BLOOMSBURY, I.B. TAURIS and the I.B. Tauris logo
are trademarks of Bloomsbury Publishing Plc

First published in Great Britain 2016
Paperback edition published 2022

Copyright © Homa Katouzian, 2022

Homa Katouzian has asserted his right under the Copyright,
Designs and Patents Act, 1988, to be identified as Author of this work.

For legal purposes the Acknowledgements on p. vii constitute
an extension of this copyright page.

All rights reserved. No part of this publication may be reproduced or
transmitted in any form or by any means, electronic or mechanical,
including photocopying, recording, or any information storage or retrieval
system, without prior permission in writing from the publishers.

Bloomsbury Publishing Plc does not have any control over, or responsibility for,
any third-party websites referred to or in this book. All internet addresses given
in this book were correct at the time of going to press. The author and publisher
regret any inconvenience caused if addresses have changed or sites have
ceased to exist, but can accept no responsibility for any such changes.

A catalogue record for this book is available from the British Library.

A catalog record for this book is available from the Library of Congress.

The publication of this book has been made possible by a
grant from the Roshan Cultural Institute.

International Library of Iranian Studies 65

ISBN: PB: 978-0-7556-4829-0
ePDF: 978-0-8577-2671-9
eBook: 978-0-8577-2965-1

Typeset by illuminati, Grosmont
Printed and bound in Great Britain

To find out more about our authors and books visit
www.bloomsbury.com and sign up for our newsletters.

In loving memory of my mother
In honour of a debt that was never repaid

Contents

PREFACE AND ACKNOWLEDGEMENTS X

INTRODUCTION   Sa'di and love   1

Expression of love
    Love's secret   31
    I was not yet born…   33
    Love at the dawn of Resurrection   35
    Lover's humility   37
    The pain of love   39
    Love and patience   41
    The turn of loving   43
    Inadequacy of reason   45
    I am just this raiment   47
    Dove and hawk   49
    I shall not repent   51
    Captive to love   53
    On his knees   55
    What fault?   57
    A tale told at every corner   59
    Let me not be   61
    Selfless love   63
    Poor reason   65
    How sweet is your poetry   67
    I am not worth the dust beneath your feet   69
    Harder than stone   71
    I still feel young   73
    No joy in living without you   75
    The heartbreak of your love   77
    When a friend is the enemy   79

Unless you cover your face 81
Only ashes beyond the burning 83
I did not invent love 85
I cannot repent of loving you 87
Let your presence light up Saʿdi's eyes 89
I've broken my vows 91
Saʿdi's name stood for loving 93
Site of Ka'ba 95
Love in spring 97
I am wonderstruck 99
Moon-face sapling 101
Trails of mystery 103

Descriptions of the beloved

...Your naked body 107
Sugar and honey 109
Miracle and grace 111
The sweetness of her mouth 113
The ruby of your lips 115
Sweet sugary lips 117
No portrayal does your face justice 119

Union

I see flowers everywhere 123
Passion for love 125
In the beloved's embrace 127
Being with the beloved 129
Discovery of a treasure 131
Engulfed in fire like Abraham 133
Your faith is yours and mine is mine 135
Night of union 137
The beloved's breast 139
Beggar and lord 141
Alchemy of love 143
In union with my lover 145

Separation

A night of loneliness 149
Separation is unbearable sorrow 151
Shattered mirror 153
Where is that dawn? 155
Always drunk 157
Prisoner of love 159
Forlorn captivity 161
Abode of the free 163
Vengeance constrained 165
Absent presence 167
Where are my drinking companions? 169
The pull of desire 171
Simorgh and the magpie 173
Ceremonies of farewell 175
I came to you like a nightingale 177
I miss you so much 179

Ethical/mystical

The place of humanity 183
The kingdom of beggars 185
Martyr to love 187
Let him fall... 189
The foundation of being 191
The same fate shall befall you 193
The world of dervishes 195

NOTES 196

INDEX OF FIRST LINES 199

Preface and acknowledgements

Sa'di was a master of the lyric, rivalled only by Hafiz and, to a lesser extent, Rumi in the annals of classical Persian poetry. Yet, strangely, he is much less admired for his lyrics than for such works as *Golestan* and *Bustan*.[1] In this volume, my fourth on Sa'di, I exclusively discuss his lyrics and present 78 of them in Persian, along with English translations, an endeavour that I hope will be appreciated by admirers of Sa'di and classical Persian poetry, as well as by lovers of lyrical poetry in any language.

In bringing this volume to its readers in an attractively designed format, I owe a considerable debt of gratitude to Dr Elahé Omidyar Mir-Djalali and the Roshan Cultural Heritage Institute, of which she is president, for their extremely generous financial support. The publication of this book in a plain format would not have been worthy of Sa'di's lyrics; it is a mark of Dr Mir-Djalali's appreciation of this great poet that when I raised this issue with her she wholeheartedly concurred. Thanks are also due to the Soudavar Memorial Foundation for its generous contribution to the cost of preparing the images by the talented artist Dr Mahbobe Ghods, which provide form and style for the lyrics and the book as a whole. I am also indebted to Mohamad Tavakoli-Targhi for his moral support and his assistance in preparing the book for publication. Finally, I humbly acknowledge my sole responsibility for any faults and shortcomings that may remain.

INTRODUCTION

Sa'di and love

Sa'di is one of the greatest classical Persian poets of all time. Born in the seventh century of Hijra, thirteenth of the Christian era, he is the only Persian luminary whose fame was so widespread that during his lifetime a Turk in Anatolia could quote his verse in a letter,[1] and shortly after whose death Chinese singers could sing one of his lyrics without knowing what it meant.[2] He was a contemporary of Rumi (though they are unlikely to have known of each other) and, despite significant differences in thought and style, influenced the poetry of Hafiz in various ways. Sa'di was translated into European languages from the seventeenth century onwards and had a considerable impact on European philosophers, intellectuals, writers and humanists in the centuries to follow. In both East and West he was most admired for his book of prose *Golestan* and, to a lesser extent, his long poem *Bustan* on morals and manners, with the result that, as noted below, they overshadowed his more than 700 lyrics and love songs, which count among the finest ever written by Persian masters.[3]

 Classical Persian literature in general and poetry in particular had come a long way since their emergence in the ninth and tenth centuries, covering a whole range of subjects, from panegyrics, lyrics, laments and reflections to history, epics, romances, meditations and mysticism.⁴ To varying degrees, the impact of this rich background can be felt throughout Sa'di's works, although both his ideas and his style are highly original.

There is a long-standing debate among Iranian as well as Western Persianist critics as to the object of love and adoration in the lyrical works of classical Persian poets, from the twelfth and, especially, the thirteenth century (the century of Sa'di and Rumi) onwards. Hardly anyone would claim that the lyricism of Rudaki Samarqandi, or Farrokhi Sistani or Manucheri Damghani, who flourished in the tenth and eleventh centuries, implied a mystical outlook and attitude. But come the twelfth century, the rise of mysticism in Persian poetry opens the gate to speculation on whether lyrical songs are addressed to a worldly and corporeal or to an other-worldly and mystical beloved. The traditional Iranian view until the twentieth century tended to favour the latter interpretation to the extent that some classicists went so far as seeking the object of love in virtually all Persian lyricism after the twelfth century in Sufi longing for reunion with the Creator. Furthermore, nineteenth- and early twentieth-century Iranian scholars tended to believe that the great Persian masters were all chaste, sexless and entirely ascetic, and that any worldly interest or passion was beneath their exalted status. Many Western scholars, although they may not have gone that far, generally tended to follow the views of Persian scholars regarding the fundamental mystical quality of much of the lyricism of the great classics. There is of course ample external evidence (leaving aside the lyric itself) in the case of poets such as the twelfth-century Sana'i and Attar, the thirteenth-century Rumi and Araqi, and the fourteenth-century Hafiz and many lesser talents in the period, supporting the description of their lyrics as mystical (though with a significant caveat in the case of Hafiz). But in what meaningful sense can so many of Sa'di's lyrics and those of the fourteenth-century Obeyd Zakani and Jahan Malak Khatun (both of whom were influenced by Sa'di), for example, be described as such? The following lines by Sa'di speak for themselves:

> The size of your mouth I will not mention
> It cannot hold even a word by intention
> Wrapped in its garment, your body
> Is just like a soul inside a body.
> And he who would see you naked
> Would say it is just a flower bed

or

> Sweeter than these lips I have not heard anyone speak
> Speak, are you sugar itself or your mouth honey?

or

> A glance at your friends much better sits
> Than sending them greetings and gifts.

or

> On reflection you'll know that your heart of steel
> Does not at all suit your breasts of silk.

or

> No-one can come between us tonight
> By the dust I swear not even a particle might.
> Stop the coquetry and pride; take off your headdress
> Open your cummerbund and let out that cypress.

or

> The beloved's breast engulfed in her curly hair
> Is like a ball of ivory hit by a black polo mallet.

It would, indeed, require a superhuman effort to interpret such lines as mystical and other-worldly. This is similarly true of many of the lyrics translated in this volume.

No classical Persian poet was a greater and more passionate lover than Sa'di. One might even claim that he was the greatest lover; he certainly stands as the greatest composer of lyrics about human love in classical Persian poetry. Nevertheless the impact of *Golestan* and *Bustan* has been so great that they have overshadowed the work of Sa'di as a poet of love songs. Not only have they seldom been translated into Western languages, in contrast to these two books, and especially *Golestan*, but even in Iran Sa'di's ghazals have never been appreciated as much as they deserve, except in vocal form in traditional Persian music.

Edward Browne believed that Sa'di was better known in Iran for his love lyrics than for *Bustan* and *Golestan*.[5] However, at the time Browne wrote this, and for a couple of decades thereafter, *Golestan* was still the basic text used by primary students to begin reading Persian. At any rate, in Iran throughout the twentieth century *Bustan* and

Golestan had pride of place over Sa'di's other works, among both scholars and the general public – leaving aside the general onslaught on Sa'di by certain 'moderns' from the mid-century, which I have discussed elsewhere.[6]

To be sure, some critical and editorial work on Sa'di's ghazals was published in the twentieth century, notably an article by the scholar and poet Rashid Yasemi in the collection *Sa'di Nameh*, which however makes the not unfamiliar, though unrealistic, claim that all of his lyrics were mystical and esoteric;[7] and the entire corpus of Sa'di's ghazals by the noted scholar and critic Mohammad Ali Forughi, which shortly afterwards was included in his edition of Sa'di's collected works, the *Kolliyat*.[8] It was decades after that when the poet and critic Habib Yaghma'i published a new edition of the lyrics.[9] In the meantime Ali Dashti, though not strictly speaking a scholar but rather an intellectual with a wide-ranging knowledge of classical Persian poetry and a flair for literary criticism, published his volume on Sa'di, which includes a small section on his lyrics, entitled 'Master of the Ghazal'.[10]

He writes that 'Sa'di is master of the ghazal. Only Hafiz does not call him master of the ghazal [whereas] all the subsequent poets have quietly thought of him as master of the ghazal and followed him.'[11] However, he further observes that 'when they wish to talk about Sa'di, first they should speak of his ghazals, but right from the beginning in this book I felt I should avoid this. On many occasions you have felt that you cannot describe your feelings... In [reading] Sa'di's ghazals we often have a feeling which we cannot express."[12]

In the twenty-first century the academic and critic Gholamhosyen Yusefi has published a new and highly annotated edition of the ghazals,[13] while the scholar Sa'id Hamidiyan has published a critical volume on Sa'di's lyrics.[14] For my part, I devote a whole chapter to Sa'di's love lyrics in my English book on his life and works,[15] as well as five critical chapters in my Persian book,[16] and include a considerable number of his ghazals in an anthology of his works.[17] The paucity of this list of largely critical editions compared with critical works on and editions of Hafiz's lyrics testifies to the relative lack of critical attention paid to Sa'di's ghazals.

The fate of Sa'di's lyrics outside Iran has been somewhat better but not that much. Sa'di's great reputation among Western intellectuals and literati, beginning in the seventeenth century but especially in the age of Enlightenment and after, largely rested on *Golestan* and, to a far lesser extent, *Bustan*, but hardly at all on his love poetry. It was the tales and wisdoms of *Golestan*, in particular, that impressed Voltaire and his fellow Encyclopédistes, to the point where Lazare Carnot, the mathematician and French revolutionary leader, named his son, a leading nineteenth-century physicist, after Sa'di, and, later, the latter's nephew, a French president, was called 'Sadi Carnot'.

Likewise, the considerable number of nineteenth-century writers and intellectuals, from Gottfried Herder,

Honoré de Balzac and Alfred de Musset through to Victor Hugo and Ernest Renan, extensively listed by Henri Massé,[18] who knew Sa'di did so not through his lyrics but on account of his other works, mainly *Golestan*. This is also largely the case with Sa'di's greatest American champion, Ralph Waldo Emerson, who, in his famous poem *Saadi*, was much more engaged with Sa'di the humanist and advocate of a positive, clean, contented outlook on life than with Sa'di the ardent lover and singer of love songs. He wrote in the introduction of a new translation of *Golestan*: 'The word *Saadi* means "fortunate". In him the trait is no result of levity, much less of convivial habit, but first of a happy nature, to which victory is habitual, easily shedding mishaps, with sensibility to pleasure, and with resources against pain. But it also results from the habitual perception of beneficent laws that control the world; he inspires in the reader a good hope.'[19]

To be sure, a fair number of the ghazals were translated into European languages in the nineteenth and early to mid-twentieth centuries. As well as some attempts in India, the prolific Austrian orientalist Joseph von Hammer Purgstall translated some of Sa'di's poems, including fourteen ghazals, and a few other German orientalists followed suit.[20] Massé's comprehensive survey for his time does not indicate the translation of any ghazals into French, and there does not seem to have been any significant change in that regard after the publication of his book in 1919. In Britain, however, a few eminent orientalists, such as E.G. Browne,[21] R.A. Nicholson[22] and A.J. Arberry,[23] tried their hands at translating a small number of the ghazals. But pride of place in this exercise – certainly in terms of sheer quantity – goes to Lucas White King, who in the 1920s published more than 600 of Sa'di's 715 lyrics.[24] Once again the paucity of critical work on Sa'di's lyrics is evident. Furthermore, what has been translated, although worthwhile, is not without certain drawbacks, especially from the standpoint of modern linguistic and literary norms. Often, words and figures of speech deployed are borrowed from the traditions of classical English poetry, which, especially in those cases close to literal translation, make comprehension difficult, and as a consequence not much is left of poems in their original form. More frequently, the formal structure of the ghazal is abandoned in favour of a prose or stanzaic style, such that, in the case of several ghazals taken together, structural consistency is lost. For these reasons the old translations are not readily accessible, quite apart from the fact that the books in which they have been published are out of print and not easily found, except in specialist libraries.

The nature and concepts of love

The theme of love is of course as old as the hills. It therefore naturally emerged in the poetry of the tenth-century classical poets writing in New Persian. But the concepts of love, lover, beloved, and so on, evolved in different ways in the period from the tenth/eleventh centuries to the thirteenth century when Sa'di flourished. First, as noted, there is hardly any major eleventh-century poet whose lyrics can truly be described as mystical. Strictly speaking, it is from the twelfth century that mystical, and more specifically Sufi, poetry began to emerge and mature in the work of such major poets as Sana'i and Attar; in the thirteenth century, in the hands of Rumi, Araqi, Shabestari, Awhadi and others, it reached its highest expression.

Second, the nature of mundane and corporeal love also began to evolve between the eleventh and thirteenth centuries: in the earlier period the lover was, if not superior, at least equal to the person he loved. The eleventh-century Farrokhi Sistani, for example, wrote of making up with his beloved 'after a long war', and the beloved bowing to him, giving the impression that in such cases the beloved was a servant or slave. In Nezami Ganjavi's romances, Khosrow and Shirin are equal as successful lovers, whereas Leyli and Majnun are also equals, though in their total failure. It is only Farhad who is selfless before the love of Shirin, the superior beloved. However, in Sa'di and hence from the thirteenth century, the lover consistently insists that he is inferior to the beloved, would do anything for so much as a glance by her, and is ready to be trampled under her feet and become talked about in town for loving her.

There may be occasional complaints about the attitude and behaviour of the beloved, her lack of response to the poor lover's begging for her attention or her lofty disregard for his pain and suffering, but all such complaints are muted, qualified and sometimes regretted, even in the same poem. Sa'di, for example, opens a ghazal by asking 'Who am I the lowly person to desire your hand?', and Hafiz (in the fourteenth century) advises in a verse 'When the beloved displays coquetry, try to offer her more'.

It is not difficult to discern the influence of mysticism and mystical love in this romantic idealisation of the object of love and the abject self-denial of the lover. Yet, at least as regards Sa'di's love poetry, matters do not simply stop there. Most of his ghazals also make obvious reference to flesh and blood, and on occasion the poet and lover indulge in the pleasures of carnal passion.

A typology of Sa'di's ghazals

Traditionally, Sa'di's ghazals were written and (later) published in his collected works under four headings: *Tayyebat*, *Badaye'*, *Khavatim* and *Ghazaliyat-e Qadim*, which titles John D. Yohannan has translated into English as 'Plain, unornamented', 'Rhetorical', 'Final' and 'Old or early'.[25] However, there is no clear justification for this categorisation, because, as Forughi has argued, the headings may not even have emanated from Sa'di himself. Indeed, in the standard edition of the collected works, cited above and used in this volume, Forughi drops the distinction among the four groups and instead divides Sa'di's ghazals into two categories: those he describes as mundane lyrics (*moghazelat*), which are the great majority, and those he places under the ethical-cum-mystical heading *mavaez*.[26]

In this volume I have divided Saʿdi's ghazals concerned with mundane or 'apparent' (*majazi*) love into four categories: those which express his love for the beloved; those which describe the beloved; those which express the joy of union; and those which reflect the sadness of separation. Inevitably, there is a degree of overlap among these four categories. However, there is enough distinction among them to justify such a typology.[27]

There remains the controversial category of Saʿdi's ghazals that are regarded as expressions of mystical, 'real' (*haqiqi*), love. It was noted above that according to Yasemi all of Saʿdi's ghazals are symbolic, esoteric and mystical, addressed to the divine beloved, much as we find in the works of Sufi poets such as Rumi, although Yasemi offers no evidence for this view. A contemporary Iranian critic, Saʾid Hamidiyan, for his part, classifies the ghazals into three groups: the obviously mundane; the obviously mystical; and the group that, though not quite mystical, 'have a mystical atmosphere'.[28] He offers several examples of the first and second groups, but only one in the third group, which is open to a wide range of interpretations.[29] One gains the impression that he regards as mundane mainly those lyrics that are intensely physical, one example of which he even describes as '"erotic", even "porno"'.[30]

The views of Saʿdi's ghazals held by Browne, Nicholson and Arberry, largely coloured as they were by the tradition of classical Iranian scholars, favour the mystical interpretation, but not without some caveats and a certain amount of ambiguity, largely arising from the stark profanity of many of the ghazals as well as the fact that Sa'di's esoteric lyrics lack the passion of the works of Sufi poets.[31] Browne, for example, suggests that, although 'the traces of [mysticism] in Sa'di's writings are neither few nor uncertain … in the main it may be said without hesitation that worldly wisdom rather than mysticism is his chief characteristic'.[32] Likewise, Nicholson, while maintaining the basic mystical interpretation, argues rather more aptly that Sa'di 'was too fine an artist to leave enthusiasm out of the picture, but "God intoxicated" is the last epithet one would think of applying to him. His poems do not suggest that he knew the higher stages of mystical life except by hearsay.'[33] Yet the problem remains that this is their view of virtually all of Sa'di's ghazals, not just those that are obviously ethical/mystical; whereas in fact upwards of 600 of the ghazals are concerned with corporeal love, and fewer than 100 are in the former category.

The upshot is that Forughi's classification, described above, is the most convincing, namely that the great majority of Sa'di's love lyrics are about human love, and the remaining small minority are ethical/mystical ghazals, which could be more aptly described as those that 'have a mystical atmosphere'.

Sa'di's enthusiasm, his passion for the love of his fellow human beings, flows through his love songs, but his ethical/mystical lyrics do not contain ecstatic outbursts such as are often observed in Rumi's ghazals, normally addressed to his mystical mentor Shams-e Tabrizi (in the image of the mystical beloved). The ghazals of Sa'di, Rumi and Hafiz are generally quite different from each other, and each of them has a unique style, although many poets subsequently adopted their models. In their hands the Persian ghazal reached its apogee.

Rumi's ghazals are often passionate in tone and have a musical metre, giving credence to reports that many were taken down by disciples while the poet uttered the words as he was 'whirling round a column'.

Sa'di's ghazals are virtually impeccable in both form and technique – being the first group of ghazals written that achieved perfection. They are about the joys of love, the ecstasy of union with the beloved and the sadness of separation, and sometimes relatively sober ethical/mystical subjects. The figures of speech or literary devices used are so masterly that the poems deploy words and generate meanings at the loftiest and most creative level, although Sa'di's ghazals are at the same time sweet in form and uncomplicated in content, such that they are not difficult to read and enjoy.

The ghazal of Hafiz is likewise formally impeccable, but it normally contains more than one theme, so that both mystical and human love as well as eulogy for an important person – notably his beloved Shah Shoja' – may be found in the same single piece. It usually combines mystical and human love so well that it is not easy to tell one from the other. Finally, in the ghazal of Hafiz, the use of relatively complex (albeit highly accomplished) metaphors and imagery – which would be further extended by the best of the 'Indian style' poets – gives it an ambiguous, sometimes even enigmatic, character, which accounts for much of the fascination experienced by readers of his poetry, including in its regular use by them in a fortune-telling context.

Here are lines from ghazals by Sa'di, Hafiz and Rumi as brief examples by which to compare their love poetry, although this exercise is inevitably partial and somewhat arbitrary:

Sa'di
I tried hard to hide the secret of desire
It was not possible to stop burning on fire.
I was alert from the start not to fall in love
All reason faded seeing your face above.
Your mouth told the ears of my soul a story
And now the people's warning is all a story.
You alone can stop the riot by hiding thy face
I cannot bear to turn away my face.
Broken-hearted, if I come to dance and wine
I'd arrive on my feet, but return shoulder-high.
Come to me in peace at night
I have not slept longing for you all night.

('Love's Secret')

Hafiz
Your beauty shone at the creation's dawn
Love appeared, on fire the entire world thrown…
Reason tried to use that fire to make a light
The lightning of disdain set the world alight
The stranger tried to come to the sight of mystery

The hidden hand stretched and put him to misery...
My celestial soul longed for the dimple of your chin
The curls of your hair it put its hand in
(Divan-e Hafiz)

Rumi
I was dead I came alive I was tears I became smile
The kingdom of love came and I became eternally alive
I have the eye of lion I have the soul of the brave
The courage of a lion, I am Venus shining bright
You do not belong here, said he, you are not insane
I went away, went mad and put myself in chains
You are not drunk, said he, not of this cut
I went and got drunk, drowned myself in delight
(Divan-e Shams)

Sa'di's ethical/mystical ghazals effectively embody a compelling mixture of reflections, guidance and admonition, but they certainly do not compare with those of the leading Sufi ghazal writers in terms of depth, enthusiasm and passion. They convey his knowledge of, respect for, and sympathy with genuine mystical thoughts and feelings, but they also show that he is not personally immersed in mystical experience. They are impeccable in form, like the rest of his poetry, and accomplished and effective in communicating their meaning, but they do not move the enthusiastic reader to heights of ecstasy and depths of passion, as does much of his mundane poetry for those moved by the fervour of love for a fellow human being. The following examples may be compared with certain Sufi ghazals, including that by Rumi quoted above.

The ghazal on the potential of humanity to rise up above the status of angels contains general mystical lessons and admonitions, but (especially in the Persian original) in a highly elevated language:

> The human body is ennobled by the human soul
> You will not be human just wearing a nice shawl
> If eye, mouth, ear and nose define a human being
> What is the difference between man and a picture
>   on the wall?
> Eating, sleeping, anger, passion are darkness and ignorance
> Animals know not of the world of humanity at all
> Try to be a human being in reality, otherwise a parrot
> May mimic the human beings' language, speech and call.
> How as a human became you captive to demons?
> Not even angels can rise up to man's potential
> If the cannibalism in your nature dies and disappears
> You will be always alive through the human soul.
>
>   ('The Place of Humanity')

The ghazal on the kingdom of beggars is more specific, though still quite familiar, pointing out the morals, attitude and behaviour that will result in mystical fulfilment and liberation. It also shows more directly the ethical and religious context within which the mystic path must take:

> There is no life as royal as that of beggars
> No kingdom is more secure than contentment
> If anyone has real dignity it is he
> Whom others treat with indignity.
> Everyone has a character, a colour, a creed
> Give them all up, that is the best thing
> On the Day of Judgement he will be clothed
> Who in this world is naked, is not adorned.

Who has real knowledge of the world?
It is he who knows no-one and is all on his own
The stone and the vegetation which are of some use
Are better than the man who is not useful to others.
You don't know, O dervish, what is expedient
Rejoice that your poverty is not inexpedient

       ('The Kingdom of Beggars')

The following ghazal combines expression of human love with elements of mystical esotericism. For that reason, as well as the fact that it contains particular themes, it anticipates a number of ghazals written by Hafiz decades later:

Trees are in bloom, nightingales drunk
The world has turned young, friends in joyful truck.
Full of charm always was our drinking partner
Now adorned, she is more charming than ever.
Those who during Ramadan broke the harp
Heard the flower breathe and broke their fast.
The lawn has been beaten down delightfully
By the mystics and non-mystics dancing joyously.
Two friends will appreciate friendship's fire
Who parted for a while then returned in full desire.
No sober person leaves the Sufis' abode [*khaneqah*]
To tell the police that the Sufis are inebriate.
In our quaint garden there is a floral tree
More balanced in figure than the cypress tree.
If the whole world becomes my enemy, I swear
By my beloved that of none other I will care.
He whom love has killed looks like seafarers
Who dropped their cargo and survived themselves.
The cypress tree was asked why it bore no fruit
The free, it replied, are empty in hand and foot.

           ('Love in Spring')

So much for Sa'di's ethical/mystical poetry as far as his lyrical songs are concerned, which are the subject of this volume. But a thoroughgoing discussion of Sa'di and mysticism would be incomplete without reference to Chapter 3 of *Bustan*, which is not a book of love lyrics but a *masnavi* on manners and morals written in the form of Ferdowsi's *Shahnameh*. It is here that, rather unexpectedly, the reader comes across some of Nicholson's 'God intoxicated' material.

Entitled 'On Love, Intoxication and Ecstasy', it is here that Sufi ideas are put forward with full force and stylistic authenticity:

> Happy the days of those longing for Him
> Whether they receive wounds or ointment from Him
> Beggars are they, having no love for kingship
> Patient in their beggary in hope of Him

Man's love of one like himself can be such as to make him forget everything but his beloved, let alone his love of the Eternal Source:

> Given that mundane love, founded on passion
> Is so potent and takes such hold
> Is it surprising that the seekers of real love
> Are so deeply submerged in its ocean?[34]

Almost the whole of Chapter 3 of *Bustan* – together with the recurring mystical and esoteric concepts and images such as Beauty, Beloved, Seeker, Friend, Truth, Candle, Moth, and so on – may be cited as evidence both of Sa'di's familiarity with Sufi concepts and categories and of his great sympathy for, if not affinity with, them. However, this subject, which has been discussed fairly extensively elsewhere, is not a concern of this volume.[35]

The question of gender

In Sa'di's lyricism regarding love of the flesh the beloved may be either a woman or a youth. Since personal pronouns are not gender-specific in the Persian language, there being a common third-person pronoun for males and females, it is not readily clear whether it is a 'he' or a 'she' to whom the poet is referring in the various poems. Yet there are often indicators that identify the gender of the beloved. In the case of women the clearest indicator is when the poet mentions their veil (*burka, niqab, purdah, hijab*), but there can be other indicators such as 'breast' and 'long hair' as well.

In the following couplet, the beloved has been likened to Shirin, Khosrow's beloved Armenian wife:

> Certainly you are the contemporary Shirin
> I am the slave of the Khosrow of the time.[36]

In this one the lover says that he will only stop watching the beloved if she puts on a veil:

> I have no intention to take my eyes off you
> Unless you stop the riot by covering your face.[37]

Here the lover refers to his being caught and exposed as the beloved's lover:

> She took the veil off my love suddenly
> The one who is hidden in a veil.[38]

In the following the lover laments the beloved wearing a veil, even a garment:

> It is a pity for that body to be covered
> It is injustice for that face to be veiled.[39]

In this couplet he compares the image of the beloved's face to morning breeze:

> Do you know why I love the morning breeze?
> It feels as if the beloved's veil has been eased.[40]

In the following couplet the beloved's face is so radiant that if she took her veil off she would shine even in daylight:

> A face which if it sheds the veil in daylight
> Will be shining like a star in a dark night.[41]

Here the beloved could hunt and capture people just by taking her veil off:

> You need no lasso for hunting people
> It is just enough if you drop the veil.[42]

In the following the beloved should wear a veil or no pious person will remain in the realm:

> If with that beauty you do not cover your face
> Never again will you see a pious person in Pars.[43]

In this one the beloved is begged to drop her veil for men and women to admire the work of God:

> Do not for God's sake hide your face from man and woman
> Let them see the work of God from left and right.[44]

This one contains a similar theme:

> I wish the veil would fall off that site of beauty
> So everyone could see the picture gallery.[45]

And finally, even the veil will not quite hide the beloved's beauty:

> The angel-face will not hide from view
> Even if she veils herself a hundred times.[46]

Love and admiration for youths are not a characteristic of Sa'di's poetry alone. The theme is found in the entire corpus of classical Persian poetry. Although it involves love for people of the same gender, this does not have quite the same personal, social and cultural implications that male homosexuality has in the West. Two types of such love may be distinguished. One is the love of Sufis and other mystics for youths purportedly as symbols of the beauty of God, as well as the expression of love, often in passionate language, for their pupils, disciples and fellow Sufis of any age. For instance, the case of Rumi's love for his mentor Shams is well known. Indeed many of his numerous ghazals are addressed to Shams and contain expressions of love for him. But he also expresses passionate love for other male friends and admirers, such as Hesam al-Din Chalabi, both in his *Masnavi* and in his ghazals.

The other kind of love for youths is devotion and admiration for the beauty, the freshness, the very youthfulness, intelligence and intellect of young male persons with whom the poet or philosopher associated as mentor, teacher, pupil and young companion. As with the first type, this love is often expressed in the language of love of women, even though it did not necessarily involve sexual relations. It corresponds to the classical Greek tradition, not to that of contemporary Western homosexuality, or to male paedophilia. Love of and admiration for academic pupils was regarded as a higher love than that for women.

Once again the gender in the love poems is not explicit because of the absence of gender-specific personal pronouns; however, in some cases there are indicators that make clear the beloved is a youth. One of these is the word *khatt*, meaning literally 'line', but representing the early growth of hair above the youth's mouth, which in full adulthood will become a moustache. It is sometimes expressed in the form of 'green line' (*khatt-e sabz*) and of 'grass of the line' (*sabzeh-ye khatt*), alluding to the colour of the early moustache in someone with dark hair. In one verse Sa'di likens the *khatt* to a line drawn by a pen that uses dust instead of ink.

Another frequently used term is *shahed*, meaning a 'witness' who is present in the company and attests to the presence of esoteric beauty; *shahed-bazi* means literally 'playing with *shahed*' – that is, love and affection for youths. Other indicative terms are *nazar* and *nazarbazi*.

Nazar means literally 'look', and *nazarbazi* 'looking-play'; *nazarbaz*, like *shahed-baz*, is one who is, or is inclined to be, involved with youths. *Saheb-nazar* means literally 'the person who looks' and has the same implication as *nazarbaz* and *shahed-baz*. All the terms refer exclusively to the love of youths. Among the great classics, these terms are found especially in the love poetry of Sa'di and of Hafiz.

Khatt

The following couplet uses the phrase 'grass of the line' to refer to the beloved's newly grown *khatt*:

> Sa'di likes the grass of the *khatt*
> Unlike animals that just love the grass.[47]

Here 'green line' is used to praise the beauty of the beloved:

> Sa'di loves a green *khatt*
> In the vicinity of a red cheek.[48]

Khatt is also used as a pun in some verses, apparently meaning 'script' or 'handwriting', but in fact meaning the youth's 'line':

> Good handwriting [*khatt*] is a chapter in your qualities
> Sweetness among your qualities is a letter in a book.[49]

Here is another example of the same pun:

> The mystics of Pars bow to your handwriting [*khatt*]
> Have you been writing a verse by Sa'di?[50]

And there are many other instances.

Shahed, nazar, nazar-bazi and *saheb-nazar*

In the following couplet the poet takes pride in his own *shahed-bazi*, his admiration and love for good-looking and intelligent youths:

> Everywhere Sa'di is known for *shahed-bazi*
> This in our creed is not a fault but an achievement.[51]

Here he advises himself to be both a recluse and a *shahed-baz*:

> Be a recluse and a *shahed-baz*, O Sa'di
> He is a *shahed* who visits the recluse.[52]

In the following couplet 'Turk' denotes a fair and light-skinned youth, and 'Frankish' means European:

> There is no *shahed* as merry as my beloved Turk
> Frankish loop is not as good as his curly hair.[53]

The following contains an excellent image:

> A *shahed* with a candle is pure riot
> Being also sleepy and drunk.[54]

In this couplet even the *mohtaseb*, the chief officer enforcing religious law, is mentioned in connection with admirers of youths:

> Mohtaseb is pursuing the libertine
> Mindless of the *shahed-baz* Sufis.[55]

The following contains the two related terms *nazar* and *shahed* in one line:

> No *shahed* that came to my sight [*nazar*] in coquetry
> Could enter my heart, for this is your place.⁵⁶

Here the first line refers to the general love of youths, but the second is about the beloved looking at the lover:

> Never in my life will I be able to stop *nazar*
> Take not your *nazar* off me O fount of beauty.⁵⁷

The same interplay of words is observed in the following couplet:

> If *nazar* is a sin, I have sinned many times
> I cannot stop myself from looking [*nazar*].⁵⁸

And there are many more such examples.

This translation

Translation of poetry from one language into another is notoriously difficult. It is perhaps more demanding in the case of classical Persian poetry than in many other traditions. Apart from the virtual loss of metre and rhyme, many of the literary devices – imagery, metaphor, punning, and so on – are also lost in the process. Yet it is possible to render classical Persian poetry in modern English such that it does not appear alien to the ordinary reader, let alone scholars of the subject.

In many, though not all, translations of Sa'di's ghazals, while the original Persian structure has often not been maintained, the rendering is close to being a literal expression of the original. The alternative to this practice, which has seldom been tried in Saʿdi's case, is a broad poetical rendering of the original verse into English poetic form, the supreme example of which is Fitzgerald's classic edition of the *Rubaiyat* of Omar Khayyam.

Here I have maintained the structure of the ghazal, such that it presents each *mesraʿ* or hemistich and *beyt* or distich in English as in the original. For example:

همه عمر بر ندارم سر از این خمار مستی
که من آن زمان نبودم که تو در دلم نشستی

Stop being drunk all my life, I will not
For I was not yet born when you entered my sight.

('I Was Not Yet Born…')

یک امشبی که در آغوش شاهد شکرم
گرم چو عود بر آتش نهند غم نخورم

This one night in my beloved's embrace
If they set me on fire it would leave no trace

('In the Beloved's Embrace')

سر آن ندارد امشب که برآید آفتابی
چه خیال ها گذر کرد و گذر نکرد خوابی

The sun does not deign to rise upon this night
What thoughts traversed the mind and no sleep in sight.

('A Night of Loneliness')

سرو قدی میان انجمنی
به که هفتاد سرو در چمنی

One with an image of the cypress tree
Is better than many real cypress trees

                                                         ('…Your Naked Body')

تن آدمی شریف است به جان آدمیت
نه همین لباس زیباست نشان آدمیت

The human body is ennobled by the human soul
You will not be human just wearing a nice shawl

                                                   ('The Place of Humanity')

The above examples, as for the most part the translations below, show that they are not broad poetical renderings of the original into English verse. Nevertheless, although not literal translations, they communicate the poet's original verse in a complementary and accessible English version. As it happens the poems selected here do not include those which are clearly addressed to a youth, and so the feminine gender has been used throughout the translation.

Classical Persian poets did not use titles for their poems, be they ghazal or any other genre. I have, however, added titles, in both Persian and English, to the ghazals translated in this volume, which generally reflect their content.

Finally, from the thirteenth century onwards each ghazal was signed by the poet in his *takhallos* or pen name. Sa'di's *takhallos* is indeed 'Sa'di' itself and is to be found at the end of each ghazal translated below.

EXPRESSION of LOVE

سر عشق

هزار جهد بکردم که سر عشق بپوشم
نبود بر سر آتش میسرم که نجوشم
بهوش بودم از اول که دل به کس نسپارم
شمایل تو بدیدم نه عقل ماند و نه هوشم
حکایتی ز دهانت به گوش جان من آمد
دگر نصیحت مردم حکایت است به گوشم
مگر تو روی بپوشی وفتنه باز نشانی
که من قرار ندارم که دیده از تو بپوشم
من رمیده دل آن به که در سماع نیایم
که گر بپای درآیم بدر برند به دوشم
بیا به صلح من امروز در کنار من امشب
که دیده خواب نکردست از انتظار تو دوشم
مرا به هیچ بدادی و من هنوز بر آنم
که از وجود تو مویی به عالمی نفروشم
به زخم خورده حکایت کنم ز دست جراحت
که تندرست ملامت کند چو من بخروشم
مرا مگوی که سعدی طریق عشق رها کن
سخن چه فایده گفتن چو پند می ننیوشم
به راه بادیه رفتن به از نشستن باطل
وگر مراد نیابم به قدر وسع بکوشم

Love's secret

I tried hard to hide the secret of desire
It was not possible to stop burning on fire.
I was alert from the start not to fall in love
All reason faded seeing your face above.
Your mouth told the ears of my soul a story
And now the people's warning is all a story.
You alone can stop the riot by hiding thy face
I cannot bear to turn away my face.
Broken-hearted, if I come to dance and wine
I'd arrive on my feet, but return shoulder-high.
Come to me in peace at night
I have not slept longing for you all night.
You gave me up for nothing, yet I am determined
Not to sell a hair of yours for earth, sky and wind.
I'll describe my pain to someone who is wounded
Telling a healthy person I'd be reprimanded.
Do not say 'Sa'di give up love and passion'
It will be no use since I will not listen.
Entering a desert is better than staying put
Even if I make it not, I'll remain on foot.[1]

که من آن زمان نبودم...
همه عمر بر ندارم سر از این خمار مستی
که من آن زمان نبودم که تو در دلم نشستی
تو نه مثل آفتابی که حضور و غیبت افتد
دگران روند و آیند و تو همچنان که هستی
چه حکایت از فراقت که نداشتم ولیکن
تو چو روی باز کردی در ماجرا ببستی
نظری به دوستان کن که هزار بار از آن به
که تحیتی نویسی و هدیتی فرستی
دل دردمند ما را که اسیر توست یارا
به وصال مرهمی نه چو به انتظار خستی
نه عجب که قلب دشمن شکنی به روز هیجا
تو که قلب دوستان را به مفارقت شکستی
برو ای فقیه دانا به خدای بخش ما را
تو و زهد و پارسایی من و عاشقی و مستی
دل هوشمند باید که به دلبری سپاری
که چو قبله ایت باشد به از آن که خود پرستی
چو زمام بخت و دولت نه به دست جهد باشد
چه کنند اگر زبونی نکنند و زیر دستی
گله از فراق یاران و جفای روزگاران
نه طریق توست سعدی، کم خویش گیر و رستی

I was not yet born...

Stop being drunk all my life, I will not
For I was not yet born when you entered my sight.
Unlike the sun you do not come and go
Others come and go; you permanently glow.
What pain I endured from our separation
Yet your face shone and ended the damnation.
A glance at your friends much better sits
Than sending them greetings and gifts.
You broke my aching heart which is your captive
With separation, now cure it with the ointment of love.
No wonder if you pierce the enemy's heart in battle
Broken as you have your friends' hearts at farewell.
Go away learned doctor, leave us to the Almighty
Us, loving and drunkenness; you, prayer and piety.
You must give your enlightened heart to love
Loving a Ka'ba is better than self-love.
Since good fortune will not be made by energy
What then can we do but show humility?
Complaining of separations and the inconstancy of life, Sa'di,
Is not in your line; take your fate and be free.[2]

صبح قیامت
در آن نفس که بمیرم در آرزوی تو باشم
بدان امید دهم جان که خاک کوی تو باشم
به وقت صبح قیامت که سر ز خاک برآرم
به گفتگوی تو خیزم به جست وجوی تو باشم
به مجمعی که در آیند شاهدان دو عالم
نظر به سوی تو دارم غلام روی تو باشم
به خوابگاه عدم گر هزار سال بخسبم
ز خواب عاقبت آگه به بوی موی تو باشم
حدیث روضه نگویم گل بهشت نجویم
جمال حور نجویم دوان به سوی تو باشم
می بهشت ننوشم ز دست ساقی رضوان
مرا به باده چه حاجت که مست روی تو باشم
هزار بادیه سهل است با وجود تو رفتن
وگر خلاف کنم سعدیا به سوی تو باشم

Love at the dawn of Resurrection

In the breath that I die, for you I'll be longing
Wishing to turn into the dust of your belonging.
At the dawn of Resurrection when my eyes open
For you I'll be looking, to you I'll be talking.
Among the beauties of the two worlds
Being a slave to your face, at you I'll be looking.
In nothingness a thousand years if I sleep
I shall rise up by the scent of your hair deep.
I'll not talk of Eden or smell the paradise rose
Or pursue the houris, to you I'll run without pause.
I will not drink of Heaven's wine, ruby bright
I will not need it, being drunk by your sight.
With you I can tread a thousand deserts with ease
Otherwise, Sa'di, I'll come to you and appease.[3]

حیف باشد که تو یار من و من یار تو باشم
من بی مایه که باشم که خریدار تو باشم
حیف باشد که تو یار من و من یار تو باشم
تو مگر سایه لطفی به سر وقت من آری
که من آن مایه ندارم که به مقدار تو باشم
خویشتن بر تو نبندم که من از خود نپسندم
که تو هرگز گل من باشی و من خار تو باشم
هرگز اندیشه نکردم که کمندت به من افتد
که من آن وقع ندارم که گرفتار تو باشم
هرگز اندر همه عالم نشناسم غم و شادی
مگرآن وقت که شادی خور و غمخوار تو باشم
گذر از دست رقیبان نتوان کرد به کویت
مگر آن وقت که در سایه زنهار تو باشم
گر خداوند تعالی به گناهیت بگیرد
گو بیامرز که من حامل اوزار تو باشم
مردمان عاشق گفتار من، ای قبله خوبان
چون نباشند که من عاشق دیدار تو باشم
من چه شایسته آنم که ترا خوانم و دانم
مگرم هم تو ببخشی که سزاوار تو باشم
گر چه دانم که به وصلت نرسم بازنگردم
که در این راه بمیرم که طلبکار تو باشم
نه در این عالم دنیا که در آن عالم عقبی
همچنان بر سر آنم که وفادار تو باشم
خاک بادا تن سعدی اگرش تو نپسندی
که نشاید که تو فخر من و من عار تو باشم

Lover's humility

Who am I, worthless me, to ask for your hand
Wrong of me to be your lover, you my beloved.
I cannot possibly rise up to your station
Unless I rise by a ray of your affection.
I will not attach myself to you for I do not
Wish at all to be your thorn and you my bud.
I never deigned to be entrapped by you
For I am not worth being a captive of you.
Sadness and joy I know not in the world
Unless I am joyful with you and sad without you.
Rivals will not let me approach your abode
Only you can protect me on the road.
If the Almighty punishes you for a sin
Tell Him that *I* am the bearer of your sins.
How could people not love listening to me
When I do so much love seeing thee?
What am I worth to want to desire you
Except if you tell me that I deserve you?
Your favours I'll not enjoy, I'll persist however
So I die in the process and become your creditor.
Not just in this but also in the other world
I shall be constant to you, and sold.
May Sa'di turn to dust if you do not like his body
Pity if I am proud of you and you ashamed of me.[4]

درد عشق

دردیست درد عشق که هیچش طبیب نیست
گر دردمند عشق بنالد عجیب نیست
دانند عاقلان که مجانین عشق را
پروای قول ناصح و پند ادیب نیست
هر کو شراب عشق نخوردست و درد درد
آنست کز حیات جهانش نصیب نیست
در مشک و عود و عنبر و امثال طیبات
خوش تر ز بوی دوست دگر هیچ طیب نیست
صید از کمند اگر بجهد بوالعجب بود
ور نه چو در کمند بمیرد عجیب نیست
گر دوست واقف است که بر من چه می رود
باک از جفای دشمن و جور رقیب نیست
بگریست چشم دشمن من بر حدیث من
فضل از غریب هست و وفا در قریب نیست
از خنده گل چنان به قفا اوفتاده باز
کو را خبر ز مشغله عندلیب نیست
سعدی ز دست دوست شکایت کجا بری
هم صبر بر حبیب که صبر از حبیب نیست

The pain of love

The pain of love is one which has no remedy
No wonder the afflicted moan of tragedy.
People of reason know that those madly in love
Listen not to the advisor and the preacher's advice.
He who's not drunk with the wine of loving
Has not experienced the joy of living.
Musk, aloes wood, ambergris, others such
None has a better aroma than my beloved much.
It's unusual for the game to break out of the trap
But it's not unusual for it to die entrapped.
If my love knew what's happening to me
I'd bear the cruelty of the rival and enemy.
My enemy's eyes wept over my fate
The stranger sympathises, the friend doesn't.
The rose is laughing with such relief
Knowing nothing of the nightingale's grief.
Sa'di, where can you complain about your beloved
Be patient with her even though she isn't.[5]

عشق و شکیبایی
دلی که عاشق و صابر بود مگر سنگ است
ز عشق تا به صبوری هزار فرسنگ است
برادران طریقت نصیحتم مکنید
که توبه در ره عشق آبگینه بر سنگ است
دگر به خفیه نمی بایدم شراب و سماع
که نیکنامی در دین عاشقان ننگ است
چه تربیت شنوم یا چه مصلحت بینم
مرا که چشم به ساقی و گوش بر چنگ است
به یادگار کسی دامن نسیم صبا
گرفته ایم و دریغا که باد در چنگ است
به خشم رفته ما را که می برد پیغام
بیا که ما سپر انداختیم اگر جنگ است
بکش چنانکه توانی که بی مشاهده ات
فراخنای جهان بر وجود من تنگ است
ملامت از دل سعدی فرونشوید عشق
سیاهی از حبشی چون رود که خودرنگ است

Love and patience

Love with patience belongs to a heart of stone
A thousand miles are between love and patience.
Stop giving me advice fellow-travellers
For repentance from love is like glass hit by stone.
I will no longer drink and dance in secret
Good name is a sin in the lovers' faith.
No lesson at all can I be taught
Seeing the cup-bearer and hearing the lute.
Thinking of you, I breathe the morning breeze
But alas it is nothing but air and wind.
Tell the beloved who's left me in anger
Even if it's war I am ready to surrender.
Come and kill me the way you know
For without you the world's nothing but a blow.
Blame will not wash love off Sa'di's heart
Black cannot be washed off someone dark.[6]

نوبت عاشقی
گفتم آهن دلی کنم چندی
ندهم دل به هیچ دلبندی
وانکه را دیده در دهان تو رفت
هرگزش گوش نشنود پندی
خاصه ما را که از ازل بودست
با تو آمیزشی و پیوندی
به دلت کز دلت بدر نکنم
سخت تر زین مخواه سوگندی
یک دم آخر حجاب یک سو نه
تا برآساید آرزومندی
همچنان پیر نیست مادر دهر
که بیاورد چون تو فرزندی
ریش فرهاد بهترک می بود
گر نه شیرین نمک پراکندی
کاشکی خاک بودمی در راه
تا مگر سایه بر من افکندی
چه کند بنده ای که از دل و جان
نکند خدمت خداوندی
سعدیا دور نیکنامی رفت
نوبت عاشقیست یکچندی

The turn of loving

I said I'd get hard-hearted awhile
Open my heart to no-one for love.
Yet he who set his eyes on your mouth
His ears will not hear any advice.
Especially a lover such as me
Having loved you from the dawn of time.
By your heart I'll keep you in my heart
Better than that I cannot swear by.
Put aside that veil just for once
To please a wishful lover at once.
The world's mother cannot be old
Of whom was born a child like you.
Farhad's love wounds would hurt him less
If Shirin did not pour so much salt on them.[7]
I wish I lay like dust on the way
So your shadow would fall on my clay.
A servant has no choice at all
Except serving his master in full.
Sa'di, the time of respectability has passed
The turn of loving has come to pass.[8]

عقل ندارد کفایتی
ای از بهشت جزوی و از رحمت آیتی
حق را به روزگار تو با ما عنایتی
گفتم نهایتی بود این درد عشق را
هر بامداد می کند از نو بدایتی
معروف شد حکایتم اندر جهان و نیست
با تو مجال آن که بگویم حکایتی
چندان که با تو غایت امکان صبر بود
کردیم و عشق را نه پدید است غایتی
فرمان عشق و عقل به یک جای نشنوند
غوغا بود دو پادشه اندر ولایتی
ز ابنای روزگار به خوبی ممیزی
چون در میان لشکر منصور رایتی
عیبت نمی کنم که خداوند امر و نهی
شاید که بنده ای بکشد بی جنایتی
زانگه که عشق دست تطاول دراز کرد
معلوم شد که عقل ندارد کفایتی
من در پناه لطف تو خواهم گریختن
فردا که هر کسی رود اندر حمایتی
درمانده ام که از تو شکایت کجا برم
هم با تو گر ز دست تو دارم شکایتی
سعدی نهفته چند بماند حدیث عشق
این ریش اندرون بکند هم سرایتی

Inadequacy of reason

You, a part of paradise and sign of bliss,
For Lord's sake of your lover take notice.
I thought there'd be an end to love's pain
Yet each morning it comes over me again.
Famous is now the story of my loving you
Though I have no chance to share it with you.
I reached the utmost limit of my patience
Alas love leaves no limit to endurance.
Love and reason cannot exist in one place
Chaos rules in a kingdom with two rulers.
In goodness you stand up among the multitude
Just like the standard of a victorious force.
Killing me without a crime is not a fault
Slaves *are* occasionally killed thus by their lord.
As soon as the army of love began its conquest
The inadequacy of reason became manifest.
Let me put myself under your protection
The day everyone is seeking redemption.
To whom could I possibly complain of you
If I must, I will have to complain to you.
Sa'di the tale of your love will not remain secret
For a wound inside will eventually surface.[9]

من این پیرهنم
تا خبر دارم از او بی خبر از خویشتنم
با وجودش ز من آواز نیاید که منم
پیرهن می بدرم دم به دم از غایت شوق
که وجودم همه او گشت و من این پیرهنم
ای رقیب این همه سودا مکن و جنگ مجوی
برکنم دیده، که من دیده از او برنکنم
خود گرفتم که نگویم که مرا واقعه ایست
دشمن و دوست بدانند قیاس از سخنم
در همه شهر فراهم ننشست انجمنی
که نه من در غمش افسانه آن انجمنم
برشکست از من و از رنج دلم باک نداشت
من نه آنم که توانم که از او برشکنم
گر همین سوز رود با من مسکین در گور
خاک اگر باز کنی سوخته یابی کفنم
گر به خون تشنه ای اینک من و سر باکی نیست
که به فتراک تو به زانکه بود بر بدنم
شرط عقل است که مردم بگریزند از تیر
من گر از دست تو باشد مژه بر هم نزنم
تا به گفتار در آمد دهن شیرینت
بیم آن است که شوری به جهان درفکنم
لب سعدی و دهانت ز کجا تا به کجا
این قدر بس که رود نام لبت بر دهنم

I am just this raiment

I've forgotten me since I've known her
She being there means that I am nowhere
I tear off my raiment a part of the excitement
That, being inside her, I'm nothing but this raiment.
Rival! Do not scheme and look for a fight
Seeing her not I'd rather tear out my eyes
Suppose I deny facing a dilemma
Friend and foe will know it from my librettos.
All and sundry know the legend of my love
My loving her is the legend of the town
She broke with me regardless that I suffer
How can I break with her, I wonder.
If they bury me with this burning flame
Open my grave and see the shroud is burnt
If you thirst for blood here take my head
It is better in your hands than on my shoulders.
People of reason run away from love's arrow
If it comes from you I will not move at all
Soon as your sweet mouth opened to talk
I am afraid my enthusiasm made me choke.
Sa'di's lips and your mouth, what a distance
I am content with my mouth mentioning your lips.[10]

کبوتر و باز
شب عاشقان بیدل چه شبی دراز باشد
تو بیا کز اول شب در صبح باز باشد
عجب است اگر توانم که سفر کنم ز دستت
به کجا رود کبوتر که اسیر باز باشد؟
ز محبتت نخواهم که نظر کنم به رویت
که محب صادق آن است که پاکباز باشد
به کرشمه ای عنایت نظری به سوی ما کن
که دعای دردمندان ز سر نیاز باشد
سخنی که نیست طاقت که ز خویشتن بپوشم
به کدام دوست گویم که محل راز باشد؟
چه نماز باشد آن را که تو در خیال باشی
تو صنم نمی گذاری که مرا نماز باشد
نه چنین حساب کردم چو تو دوست می گرفتم
که ثنا و مدح گوییم و جفا و ناز باشد
دگرش چو باز بینی غم دل مگوی سعدی
که شب وصال کوتاه و سخن دراز باشد
قدمی که برگرفتی به وفا و عهد یاران
اگر از بلا بترسی قدم مجاز باشد

Dove and hawk

The night of selfless lovers is too long
Come my love so we'll have morning from the start.
There's nowhere I'd be able to run from you
Where can a dove go from the claws of a hawk?
So deep is my love that I bear not to see your face
A selfless lover must after all be honest.
Do throw a glance at me by a kind gesture
Since it's necessity that makes sufferers pray.
The word that I cannot bear to hide from myself
To whom shall I take it to keep as a secret?
With you in mind my ritual prayer is void
The idol in you stops me saying it at all.
I did not reckon, when seeking your love,
That while I adore you, you will not care.
Next time you see her, Sa'di, don't open your heart
For the night of union is short, and the talk long.
The step you take towards the beloved
Will be false if you are afraid of a bad end.[11]

من توبه نمی کنم

گر من ز محبتت بمیرم
دامن به قیامتت بگیرم
از دنیی و آخرت گزیر است
وز صحبت دوست ناگزیرم
ای مرهم ریش دردمندان
درمان دگر نمی پذیرم
آن کس که به جز تو کس ندارد
در هر دو جهان، من آن فقیرم
ای محتسب از جوان چه خواهی؟
من توبه نمی کنم که پیرم
یک روز کمان ابروانش
می بوسم و گو بزن به تیرم
ای باد بهار عنبرین بوی
در پای لطافت تو میرم
چون می گذری به خاک شیراز
گو من به فلان زمین اسیرم
در خواب نمی روم که بی دوست
پهلو نه خوش است با حریرم
ای مونس روزگار سعدی
رفتی و نرفتی از ضمیرم

I shall not repent

If I die of your love in this world
I'll hold you to account in the next world
One can choose between this and the other world
But I have no choice other than my beloved.
You are a remedy to everyone's ills
No remedy except your love please
He who has no-one but you in the two worlds
Is me, the poor beggar among all.
Religious police stop troubling the young!
Even *I* will not repent being old, not young
One day I'll kiss the bows of her eyebrows
And then I'll be ready to kiss her arrows.
Tell the fragrant spring breeze
For whose tenderness I am ready to die
To tell my love when passing through Shiraz
That your lover is captive in some other place.
I am sleepless because without my beloved
Beside me, I cannot even rest in a silk bed
Sweet beloved of Sa'di's entire life!
You are gone, but are still on my mind.[12]

شهربند عشق
هر شب اندیشه دیگر کنم و رای دگر
که من از دست تو فردا بروم جای دگر
بامدادن که برون می‌نهم از منزل پای
حسن عهدم نگذارد که نهم پای دگر
هر کسی را سر چیزی و تمنای کسیست
ما به غیر از تو نداریم تمنای دگر
زانکه هرگز به جمال تو در آیینه وهم
متصور نشود صورت و بالای دگر
وامقی بود که دیوانه عذرایی بود
منم امروز و تویی، وامق و عذرای دگر
وقت آن است که صحرا گل و سنبل گیرد
خلق بیرون شده هر قوم به صحرای دگر
بامدادان به تماشای چمن بیرون آی
تا فراغ از تو نماند به تماشای دگر
هر صباحی غمی از دست زمان پیش آید
گویم این نیز نهم بر سر غم‌های دگر
باز گویم که نه دوران حیات این همه نیست
سعدی امروز تحمل کن و فردای دگر

Captive to love

Every day and night I almost decide
To give up your love and leave town
Yet as soon as I set foot out of my home
Constancy stops me from leaving you alone.
They all desire something or someone
Other than you, I desire no-one
Because not even in the mirror of illusion
Will one as beautiful as you enter the imagination.
In legend Vameq was mad about Azra
I am now another Vameq, and you another Azra
It is the season of rose and nightingale
Everyone is outdoors to enjoy the air.
Come in the morning to see the green grass
So I will not see it away from your pass
Each day I am seized by the sadness of love
I say let's load this upon what's already gone.
But then I say no, Sa'di, life is short
Try to put up with it more and more.[13]

در دامنت آویزد
هشیار کسی باید کز عشق بپرهیزد
وین طبع که من دارم با عقل نیامیزد
آن کس که دلی دارد آراسته معنی
گر هر دو جهان باشد در پای یکی ریزد
گر سیل عقاب آید شوریده نیندیشد
ور تیر بلا بارد دیوانه نپرهیزد
آخر نه منم تنها در بادیه سودا
عشق لب شیرینت بس شور برانگیزد
بی بخت چه غم سازم تا برخورم از وصلت؟
بی مایه زبون باشد هر چند که بستیزد
فضل است اگرم خوانی، عدل است اگرم رانی
قدر تو نداند آن کز زجر تو بگریزد
تا دل به تو پیوستم راه همه در بستم
جایی که تو بنشینی بس فتنه که برخیزد
سعدی نظر از رویت کوته نکند هرگز
ور روی بگردانی در دامنت آویزد

On his knees

Careful is one who shuns the lovers' season
Alas my nature cannot bear the coldness of reason.
He whose heart is adorned with pure truth
Will deliver both worlds to the one he adores.
A flood of eagles will not frighten a lover
Just as a rain of arrows will not deter a mad fighter.
I am after all not alone in the realm of compassion
The love of your sweet lips also raises passion.
My bad luck does not allow me to have you
Hard as he tries, what can a poor man do?
Taking me will be virtuous, rejecting me just
He is not a true lover who runs from your wrath.
Since I've come to you all doors are shut
Wherever you are, riot breaks out.
Sa'di will not stop staring at your face
And will hold your lap if you turn your face.[14]

کدام عیب؟
کس این کند که دل از یار خویش بردارد؟
مگر کسی که دل از سنگ سخت تر دارد
که گفت من خبری دارم از حقیقت عشق
دروغ گفت گر از خویشتن خبر دارد
اگر نظر به دو عالم کند حرامش باد
که از صفای درون با یکی نظر دارد
هلاک ما به بیابان عشق خواهد بود
کجاست مرد که با ما سر سفر دارد
گر از مقابله شیر آید از عقب شمشیر
نه عاشق است که اندیشه از خطر دارد
وگر بهشت مصور کنند عاشق را
به غیر دوست نشاید که دیده بردارد
از آن متاع که در پای دوستان ریزند
مرا سریست ندانم که او چه سر دارد؟
دریغ پای که بر خاک می نهد معشوق
چرا نه بر سر و بر چشم ما گذر دارد؟
عوام عیب کنندم که عاشقی سعدی
کدام عیب که سعدی خود این هنر دارد
نظر به روی تو انداختن حرامش باد
که جز تو در همه عالم کسی دگر دارد

What fault?

Would anyone give up loving his sweetheart?
He would who has a heart stone-hard
The lover who claims to know true love
Lies if he cares at all for his own self.
He who is in love from the bottom of his heart
Cannot love anything else, even the two worlds
Our death is surely in the wilderness of love
What gallant man will keep us company?
If lions come from the front, swords from behind,
He is not a true lover who would for a second mind
And if they bring paradise itself before his eyes
The true lover will not take his eyes off his beloved.
I only have my head to put at my sweetheart's feet
And I wonder what *she* will think of it
Sadly, she rambles on plain dust
I wish she'd walk on me if she must.
The ignorant blame Sa'di's fault for love
This is not a fault but an asset that I've got
Anyone who has anyone but you
Does not at all deserve to love you.[15]

داستانیست که بر هر سر بازاری هست
مشنو ای دوست که غیر از تو مرا یاری هست
یا شب و روز به جز فکر توام کاری هست
به کمند سر زلفت نه من افتادم و بس
که به هر حلقه موییت گرفتاری هست
گر بگویم که مرا با تو سر و کاری نیست
در و دیوار گواهی بدهد کاری هست
هر که عیبم کند از عشق و ملامت گوید
تا ندیدست ترا بر منش انکاری هست
صبر بر جور رقیبت چه کنم گر نکنم؟
همه دانند که در صحبت گل خاری هست
نه من خام طمع عشق تو می ورزم و بس
که چو من سوخته در خیل تو بسیاری هست
باد خاکی ز مقام تو بیاورد و ببرد
آب هر طیب که در کلبه عطاری هست
من چه در پای تو ریزم که پسند تو بود
جان و سر را نتوان گفت که مقداری هست
من از این دلق مرقع بدرآیم روزی
تا همه خلق بدانند که زناری هست
همه را هست همین داغ محبت که مراست
که نه مستم من و در دور تو هشیاری هست
عشق سعدی نه حدیثیست که پنهان ماند
داستانیست که بر هر سر بازاری هست

A tale told at every corner

Do not believe, my love, that I have any other
Or that day and night about anything else I bother.
I was caught in the lasso of your long hair
Like others entrapped in its every curl.
Suppose I pretend not to care about you
The whole world will bear witness that I do.
He who blames me for being in love
Will stop it when he sets eyes on you my love.
I'll bear the oppression of my rival for loving you
Wanting a flower, one must bear its thorns too.
I am not the only one who longs for you
Multitudes have been burnt in your milieu.
When the wind blows the dust from your home
Its fragrance fills the air better than perfume.
What shall I offer you that may please you?
I cannot claim that my life is worthy of you.
One day I shall take off my patched raiment
So all will see the cross which I wear under it.
We all suffer from bearing the brand of your love
I am not the only drunk; there is hardly a sober one.
Sa'di's love is not such that can be under cover
It is a tale that they tell at every corner.[16]

ببرم بار گرانت

چه لطیف است قبا بر تن چون سرو روانت
آه اگر چون کمرم دست رسیدی به میانت
در دلم هیچ نیاید مگر اندیشه وصلت
تو نه آنی که دگر کس بنشیند به مکانت
گر تو خواهی که یکی را سخن تلخ بگویی
سخن تلخ نباشد چو برآید به دهانت
نه من انگشت نمایم به هواداری رویت
که تو انگشت نمایی و خلایق نگرانت
در اندیشه ببستم قلم وهم شکستم
که تو زیباتر از آنی که کنم وصف و بیانت
سرو را قامت خوب است و قمر را رخ زیبا
تو نه آنی و نه اینی، که هم این است و هم آنت
ای رقیب ار نگشایی در دلبند به رویم
این قدر باز نمایی که دعا گفت فلانت
من همه عمر بر آنم که دعاگوی تو باشم
گر تو باشی که نباشم تن من برخی جانت
سعدیا چاره ثبات است و مدارا و تحمل
من که محتاج تو باشم ببرم بار گرانت

Let me not be
How soft is the garment on your figure
How I wish I could embrace you like your belt
Naught can I think of but having you
For no-one can ever compete with you.
If you speak of anyone with bitterness
It'll not be bitter as it leaves your lips
Not only am I notorious for loving you
You too are notorious, with multitudes watching you.
I've stopped thinking and given up all illusion
For you are too beautiful to locate in a vision
The moon's pretty, the cypress tree is elegant
You are neither as you are like them both.
O rival if you stop me from seeing her
Tell her at least that I prayed for her
All my life, my love, I'll pray for you to be
If your existence excludes mine, let it be.
There's no choice, Sa'di, but forbearance
Now that you need her, bear it with patience.[17]

عشق بی خود
مرا خود با تو چیزی در میان هست
وگرنه روی زیبا در جهان هست
وجودی دارم از مهرت گدازان
وجودم رفت و مهرت همچنان هست
مبر ظن کز سرم سودای عشقت
رود، تا بر زمینم استخوان هست
اگر پیشم نشینی دل نشانی
وگر غایب شوی در دل نشان هست
بگفتن راست ناید شرح حسنت
ولیکن گفت خواهم تا زبان هست
ندانم قامت است آن یا قیامت
که می گوید چنین سرو روان هست
توان گفتن به مه مانی ولی ماه
نپندارم چنین شیرین دهان هست
بجز پیشت نخواهم سر نهادن
اگر بالین نباشد آستان هست
برو سعدی که کوی وصل یاران
نه بازاریست کانجا قدر جان هست

Selfless love

For you I feel something, something special
And not just because you look pretty.
My whole being is burning with your love
I have ceased to be, but there still is your love.
Do not believe that I will leave you alone
For as long as in my body there is a bone.
Come, and you will live in my heart
Go, and you'll be remembered by it.
No tongue can quite describe your beauty
But as long as I have a tongue it'll be my duty.
The beauty of your figure is a source of wonder,
It proves that there are moving cypress trees.
Your face may be likened to the moon
But the moon cannot speak sweet words.
I will not rest next to anyone but you
At your feet, if not on your pillow.
Give up, Sa'di, for in the bazaar of love
They do not put any value on men's life.[18]

عقل بیچاره
زانگه که بر آن صورت خوبم نظر افتاد
از صورت بی طاقتی ام پرده برافتاد
گفتیم که عقل از همه کاری بدرآید
بیچاره فرو ماند چو عشقش بدر افتاد
شمشیر کشیدست نظر بر سر مردم
چون پای بدارم که ز دستم سپر افتاد؟
در سوخته پنهان نتوان داشتن آتش
ما هیچ نگفتیم و حکایت بدر افتاد
با هر که خبر گفتم از اوصاف جمیلش
مشتاق چنان شد که چو من بی خبر افتاد
هان تا لب شیرین نستاند دلت از دست
کان کز غم او کوه گرفت از کمر افتاد
صاحب‌نظران این نفس گرم چو آتش
دانند که در خرمن من بیشتر افتاد
نیکم نظر افتاد بر آن منظر مطبوع
کاول نظرم هر چه وجود از نظر افتاد
سعدی نه حریف غم او بود ولیکن
با رستم دستان بزند هر که درافتاد

Poor reason

Ever since I set eyes on that beautiful face
It became clear that I had lost patience
I had thought that reason could cope
Poor reason lost out to love's onslaught.
She's drawn the dagger of love on her lovers
I have dropped the shield and am defenceless
You cannot hide fire in what is burning
My love was thus exposed without a warning.
Whoever I told about her wonderful aspects
Fell for her and like me became unconscious
Be careful that you do not fall for the lips of Shirin
For even a hero like Farhad they brought down.
The enlightened know that her fiery breath
Set fire to my harvest more than others
The minute I saw that garden of beauty
I could not possibly watch another body.
Sa'di could not bear the sadness of her love
Which you must be a Rostam to be able to fight.[19]

اندازه ندارد که چه شیرین سخنی
پیش رویت دگران صورت بر دیوارند
نه چنین صورت و معنی که تو داری دارند
تا گل روی تو دیدم همه گلها خارند
تا ترا یار گرفتم همه خلق اغیارند
آن که گویند به عمری شب قدری باشد
مگر آن است که با دوست به پایان آرند
دامن دولت جاوید و گریبان امید
حیف باشد که بگیرند و دگر بگذارند
نه من از دست نگارین تو مجروحم و بس
که به شمشیر غمت کشته چو من بسیارند
عجب از چشم تو دارم که شبانگه تا روز
خواب می گیرد و شهری ز غمت بیدارند
بوالعجب واقعه ای باشد و مشکل دردی
که نه پوشیده توان گفت نه گفتن یارند
یعلم الله که خیالی ز تنم بیش نماند
بلکه آن نیز خیالیست که می پندارند
سعدی اندازه ندارد که چه شیرین سخنی
باغ طبعت همه مرغان شکرگفتارند
تا به بستان ضمیرت گل معنی بشکفت
بلبلان از تو فرومانده چو بوتیمارند

How sweet is your poetry
Beside your face others are pictures on the wall
None has the face and depth of you at all
With the flower of your face all flowers are thistles
Having taken you as friend all others are strangers.
They say one night of life is the Sacred Night
It must be the night that is spent at your side
It'll be a pity to sacrifice amorous success
To any and all things else.
With your lovely hands you've not just injured me
Killed like me by your sabre are many
I am astonished at your eye that every night
Falls asleep while a whole town is awake for your love.
It's something strange, a difficult pain
That can be neither hidden nor explained
God knows that I am nothing but your thought
Although even that is far from thought.
Sa'di, your words are sweeter than sugar
The garden of your poetry is filled with singing birds
Ever since roses have sprouted in your mind's garden
Nightingales have lost the art of competition.[20]

خاک بازار نیرزم

بخت آیینه ندارم که در او می نگری
خاک بازار نیرزم که بر او می گذری
من چنان عاشق رویت که ز خود بی خبرم
تو چنان فتنه خویشی که ز ما بی خبری
به چه مانند کنم در همه آفاق ترا
کانچه در وهم من آید تو از آن خوب تری
برقع از پیش چنین روی نشاید برداشت
که به هر گوشه چشمی دل خلقی ببری
دیده ای را که به دیدار تو دل می نرود
هیچ علت نتوان گفت مگر بی بصری
به فلک می رود آه سحر از سینه ما
تو همی بر نکنی دیده ز خواب سحری
خفتگان را خبر از محنت بیداران نیست
تا غمت پیش نیاید غم مردم نخوری
هر چه در وصف تو گویند به نیکویی هست
عیب آنست که هر روز به طبعی دگری
گر تو از پرده برون آیی و رخ بنمایی
پرده از کار همه پرده نشینان بدری
عذر سعدی ننهد هر که ترا نشناسد
حال دیوانه نداند که ندیدست پری

I am not worth the dust beneath your feet

My luck is not a mirror at which you may look
My person is not worth the dust on which you may walk
I love you so much that I have forgotten me
You are so full of yourself that you are unaware of me.
To what can I liken you in the whole world
For you are better than anything in my thought
He is surely struck by a fit of blindness
Who does not lose himself on seeing your face.
I thought I would leave town to forget you
But I cannot, since I see you everywhere I go
Our sighs rise up to the skies at dawn
You will not even open your eyes at dawn.
Sleepers are unaware of the pain of the sleepless
For a carefree person does not sense the cares of others
All that they say in your praise is right
Except that you keep changing your mind.
If you remove the purdah and show your face
You will expose the secrets of all purdah-dwellers
Those who do not know you will admonish Saʻdi:
A madman is blamed by those who are not bewitched.[21]

سخت تر از سنگ
گر کنم در سر وفات سری
سهل باشد زیان مختصری
ای که قصد هلاک من داری
صبر کن تا ببینمت نظری
نه حرام است در رخ تو نظر
که حرام است چشم بر دگری
دوست دارم که خاک پات شوم
تا مگر بر سرم کنی گذری
متحیر نه در جمال توام
عقل دارم به قدر خود قدری
حیرتم در صفات بی چون است
کاین کمال آفرید در بشری
ببری هوش و طاقت زن و مرد
گر تردد کنی به بام و دری ...
آه سعدی اثر کند در کوه
نکند در تو سنگدل اثری
سنگ را سخت گفتمی همه عمر
تا بدیدم ز سنگ سخت تری

Harder than stone

It would be but a small loss
To lose my head for your love
Since you are bent on killing me
Let me at least see you for a while.
Looking at your face is not forbidden [haram]
It's looking at another that's forbidden
I wish to turn into dust at your threshold
So that you would step on my head.
I am not puzzled by your beauty
Since I do have some sense in me
I am puzzled at God's qualities
That created such a perfect being.
Anyone anywhere who sets eyes on thee
Will be lost by your dazzling beauty…
Even hills are affected by Saʻdi's sigh
Alas, it has no effect on your stone heart.
All my life I said stones were hard, unawares
That some hearts may be harder than stones."[22]

همچنان طبعم جوانی می کند
هر که بی او زندگانی می کند
گر نمی میرد گرانی می کند
من بر آن بودم که ندهم دل به عشق
سروبالا دلستانی می کند
مهربانی می نمایم بر قدش
سنگدل نامهربانی می کند
برف پیری می نشیند بر سرم
همچنان طبعم جوانی می کند
ماجرای دل نمی گفتم به خلق
آب چشمم ترجمانی می کند
آهن افسرده می کوبد که جهد
با قضای آسمانی می کند
عقل را با عشق زور پنجه نیست
احتمال از ناتوانی می کند
چشم سعدی در امید روی یار
چون دهانش درفشانی می کند
هم بود شوری در این سر بی خلاف
کاین همه شیرین زبانی می کند

I still feel young

He who lives without her
And does not die is obdurate.
I was determined to avoid loving
It is she who did the enticing.
I am worshipping her body
Stone-hearted, she ignores me.
My head is turning snow white
But I still feel just as young.
I would not have opened up my heart
But I was exposed by the tears in my eyes.
He who struggles against his fate
Is beating iron with his head.
Reason cannot overcome love
It just hopelessly tries.
Longing to see her, Sa'di's eyes
Drop pearls as does her mouth.
He must indeed be full of passion
Who has such a sweet expression.[23]

عیش را بی تو عیش نتوان گفت
زنده بی دوست خفته در وطنی
مثل مرده ایست در کفنی
عیش را بی تو عیش نتوان گفت
چه بود بی وجود روح تنی؟
تا صبا می رود به بستان ها
چون تو سروی نیافت در چمنی
و آفتابی خلاف امکان است
که بر آید ز جیب پیرهنی
وآن شکن بر شکن قبایل زلف
که بلاییست زیر هر شکنی
بر سر کوی عشق بازاریست
که نیارد هزار جان ثمنی
جای آن است اگر ببخشایی
که نبینی فقیرتر ز منی
هفت کشور نمی کنند امروز
بی مقالات سعدی انجمنی
از دو بیرون نه: یا دلت سنگ است
یا به گوشت نمی رسد سخنی

No joy in living without you

Sleeping in an abode without the beloved
Is just like a dead person wrapped in a shroud
Living cannot be called living without you
For what worth is a body without a soul?
Ever since the morning passed through the fields
I have not found a cypress tree like you indeed
And it is unbelievable that the sun
Would rise from an open-necked gown.
And there is that chain of your long hair
Which hides a sedition under each of its curls
In the streets of love there is a bazaar
Where a thousand lives are not worth a dime.
I really deserve to receive your alms
For you will find none poorer than me likewise
Today no groups gather in the seven realms
Where they do not recite Sa'di's Persian pearls.
Either you have a heart made of stone
Or my pleas don't reach your ears at all.[24]

بلای عشق تو

نرفت تا تو برفتی خیالت از نظرم
برفت در همه عالم به بی دلی خبرم
نه بخت و دولت آنم که با تو بنشینم
نه صبر و طاقت آنم که از تو درگذرم
من از تو روی نخواهم به دیگری آورد
که زشت باشد هر روز قبله دگرم
بلای عشق تو بر من چنان اثر کردست
که پند عالم و عابد نمی کند اثرم
قیامتم که به دیوان حشر پیش آرند
میان آن همه تشویش در تو می نگرم
به جان دوست که چون دوست در برم باشد
هزار دشمن اگر بر سرند غم نخورم
نشان پیکر خوبت نمی توانم داد
که در تامل او خیره می شود بصرم
تو نیز اگر نشناسی مرا عجب نبود
که هر چه در نظر آید از آن ضعیفترم
به جان و سر که نگردانم از وصال تو روی
وگر هزار ملامت رسد به جان و سرم
مرا مگوی که سعدی چرا پریشانی
خیال روی تو بر می کند به یکدگرم

The heartbreak of your love

I still think of you even if you care not
The whole world has learned of my lonely lot
Neither do I have the luck to be with you
Nor the patience to forget about you.
I cannot leave you for anyone anyway
Since I cannot have a Ka'ba every day
The heartbreak of your love has struck me such
That no amount of advice can make me give up.
At the Resurrection when they bring me to the book
Amidst all the fear for you I will still look
I swear by my friend that when she is with me
I will not worry even if I have a thousand enemies.
I cannot possibly say how fine is your body
Since I keep gazing at it instead of looking
And no wonder if you too do not recognise me
Since I am much less than anyone can be.
I'll not stop seeking you, by my life and mind,
Even if my life and mind are showered with reprimand
Do not ask me, 'Sa'di, why are you despondent?'
It's because the thought of you turns my temperament.[25]

چون دوست دشمن است

بگذار تا مقابل روی تو بگذریم
دزدیده در شمایل خوب تو بنگریم
شوق است در جدایی و جور است در نظر
هم جور به که طاقت شوقت نیاوریم
روی ار به روی ما نکنی حکم از آن توست
باز آ که روی در قدمانت بگستریم
ما را سریست با تو که گر خلق روزگار
دشمن شوند و سر برود هم بر آن سریم
گفتی ز خاک بیشترند اهل عشق من
از خاک بیشتر نه که از خاک کمتریم
ما با تو ایم و با تو نه ایم اینت بولعجب
در حلقه ایم با تو و چون حلقه بر دریم
نه بوی مهر می شنویم از تو ای عجب
نه روی آنکه دگر کس بپروریم
از دشمنان برند حکایت به دوستان
چون دوست دشمن است شکایت کجا بریم؟
ما خود نمی رویم دوان از قفای کس
آن می برد که ما به کمند وی اندریم
سعدی تو کیستی که در این حلقه کمند
چندان فتاده اند که ما صید لاغریم

When a friend is the enemy

Do let me pass by your face
And steal a look from that beautiful space
Separation brings longing, but seeing hurts
I like the hurt since I cannot bear to wait.
It is your privilege not to look at my face
At least step on my face for God's sake
My head is at your feet and even if enemies
Cut it off it will still be there, at your feet.
You said your lovers are more than dust
Not more, we are in fact less than dust
Strange that I am both with you and without you
Apparently one with you and yet far from you.
I neither receive the fragrance of love from you
Nor have the courage to choose someone to replace you
They complain of their enemies to their friends
When a friend is the enemy, to whom shall I protest?
I am not running after her by my own free will
I am caught in her lasso and pulled without help
Sa'di in the loop of this lasso are prisoners
Beside whom you are but an insignificant game.[26]

مگر تو روی بپوشی

کسی که روی تو دیدست حال من داند
که هرکه دل به تو پرداخت صبر نتواند
مگر تو روی بپوشی وگر نه ممکن نیست
که آدمی که تو بیند نظر بپوشاند
هر آفریده که چشمش بر این جمال افتاد
دلش ببخشد و بر جانت آفرین خواند
اگر به دست کند باغبان چنین سروی
چه جای چشمه که بر چشمهاش بنشاند
چه روزها به شب آورد جان منتظرم
ببوی آنکه شبی با تو روز گرداند
به چند حیله شبی در فراق روز کنم
وگر نبینمت آن روز هم به شب ماند
جفا و سلطنتت می رسد ولی مپسند
که گر سوار براند پیاده در ماند
به دست رحمتم از خاک آستان بردار
که گر بیفکنیم کس به هیچ نستاند
چه حاجت است به شمشیر قتل عاشق را
حدیث دوست بگویش که جان برافشاند
پیام اهل دل است این خبر که سعدی داد
نه هر که گوش کند معنی سخن داند

Unless you cover your face

He who has seen your face would know how I feel
Since anyone who fell in love with you could not sit still
It is impossible to take one's eyes off your face
Unless you cover it and thus hide your face.
Anyone whose eyes fell on that beauty
Would heartily admire your whole being
If the gardener tries to plant such a cypress tree
He would plant it not in a spring but in his own eye.
How many nights my longing ended in day
In the hope that I spend a night with you till day
I try to bring the night of separation somehow to day
But it turns into night when I don't see you on the day.
I endure your unkindness and royal pride
But do not let the horse ride and the pawn stay behind.
Take me off the dust with your blessed hand
Since if you don't no-one will give me a hand
What use is killing a lover with the sword of love?
Tell him, instead, the story of love so his spirits lift up.
This was a message from lovers which Sa'di brought
Though it will not give any listener food for thought.[27]

اکنون که بسوختش خطر نیست
گر صبر دل از تو هست و گر نیست
هم صبر که چاره دگر نیست
ای خواجه به کوی دلستانان
زنهار مرو که ره به در نیست
دانند جهانیان که در عشق
اندیشه عقل معتبر نیست
گویند به جانبی دگر رو
وز جانب او عزیزتر نیست
گرد همه بوستان بگشتیم
بر هیچ درخت از این ثمر نیست
من در خور تو چه تحفه آرم؟
جان است و بهای یک نظر نیست
دانی که خبر ز عشق دارد؟
آن کز همه عالمش خبر نیست
سعدی چو امید وصل باقیست
اندیشه جان و بیم سر نیست
پروانه ز عشق بر خطر بود
اکنون که بسوختش خطر نیست

Only ashes beyond the burning

Whether or not my heart is patient in loving
Let it be patient for there is no other remedy.
Friend, try not to go to where loved ones live
For you will find no possible way out of it
They all know in the world that in loving
There is no room at all for reasoning.
They tell me to seek another lover
But no-one is as adorable as her
I have explored the whole of the orchard
But no tree bears fruit quite like the beloved.
What gift worthy of you can I bring you?
For I have just a life which is not worth a look by you
Do you know who really understands love?
He who is completely unaware of the world.
Sa'di, since you still hope for a union
Fear not of losing your life for it brings no fear
The loving moth was in danger of the candle's wrath
Now that the candle has burnt it the danger has passed.[28]

عشق اختراع من نبود
عشقبازی نه من آخر به جهان آوردم
یا گناهیست که اول من مسکین کردم
تو که از صورت حال دل ما بی خبری
غم دل با تو نگویم که ندانی دردم
ای که پندم دهی از عشق و ملامت گویی
تو نبودی که من این جام محبت خوردم
تو برو مصلحت خویشتن اندیش که من
ترک جان دادم از این پیش که دل بسپردم
عهد کردیم که جان در سر کار تو کنیم
وگر این عهد به پایان نبرم نامردم
من که روی از همه عالم به وصالت کردم
شرط انصاف نباشد که بمانی فردم
راست خواهی تو مرا شیفته می گردانی
گرد عالم به چنین روز نه من می گردم
خاک نعلین تو ای دوست نمی یارم شد
تا بر آن دامن عصمت ننشیند گردم
روز دیوان جزا دست من و دامن تو
تا بگویی دل سعدی به چه جرم آزردم

I did not invent love

Loving, after all, was not my invention
Nor sinning that miserable I first committed
I will not tell you about the pain in my heart
Since you do not even know what is in my heart.
O Preacher who scolds me for loving
Where were you when I drank the wine of loving?
You go and think what's best for your life
Since I gave up my life the minute I fell in love.
I pledged my life to the love of my lover
If I break it I will not be a man worthy of love
I turned away from the whole world for having you
It will not be fair if you keep me longing for you.
It was you who sent me round the world bewitched
I am not running round the world of my own free will
I dare not wish to turn into the dust of your shoes, beloved
Lest as dust I would pollute your clean, sinless garment.
In the Day of Judgement I'll hold your hand
And ask why you hurt Sa'di's heart in this world.[29]

که من از عشق توبه نتوانم

بس که در منظر تو حیرانم
صورتت را صفت نمی دانم
پارسایان ملامتم مکنید
که من از عشق توبه نتوانم
هر که بینی به جسم و جان زنده ست
من به امید وصل جانانم
به چه کار آید این بقیت جان
که به معشوق بر نیفشانم؟
گر تو از من عنان بگردانی
من به شمشیر برنگردانم
گر بخوانی مقیم درگاهم
ور برانی مطیع فرمانم
من نه آنم که سست بازآیم
ور ز سختی به لب رسد جانم
گر اجابت کنی وگر نکنی
چاره من دعاست، می خوانم
سهل باشد صعوبت ظلمات
گر به دست آید آب حیوانم
تا کی آخر جفا بری سعدی؟
چه کنم پای بند احسانم
کار مردان تحمل است و سکون
من کیم؟ خاک پای مردانم

I cannot repent of loving you

I am so bewitched by your look
That I cannot describe how you look
I just cannot repent of loving
Let the pious keep scolding.
People live by their bodies and souls
And I, by being with her body and soul,
No use would be for what life I have left
Except if I give it to the one close to my chest.
If you turn the rein away from me my love
Not even a sword could turn me away from love
If you summon me, I'll be ready at your feet
And if you reject me I'll be your obedient servant.
I am not one who would lightly go away
Even if I am driven to the point of death
Whether you accept me or let me go
My only hope will be praying for you.
In pitch dark it is difficult to see
But it's easy, looking for that immortal beauty
Till when, Sa'di, will you bear unkindness?
Perhaps till you die with lovesickness.
Real men are at peace and tolerate hardship
Who am I? The dust of real men's feet.[30]

قدم بر دو چشم سعدی نه
به کوی لاله رخان هر که عشقباز آید
امید نیست که دیگر به عقل بازآید
کبوتری که دگر آشیان نخواهد دید
قضا همی بردش تا به چنگ باز آید
ندانم ابروی شوخت چگونه محرابیست
که گر ببیند زندیق در نماز آید
بزرگوار مقامی و نیکبخت کسی
که هر دم از در او چون تویی فراز آید
ترش نباشم اگر صد جواب تلخ دهی
که از دهان تو شیرین و دلنواز آید
بیا و گونه زردم ببین و نقش بخوان
که گر حدیث کنم قصه ای دراز آید
خروشم از تف سینه است و ناله از سر درد
نه چون دگر سخنان کز سر مجاز آید
به جای خاک قدم بر دو چشم سعدی نه
که هر که چون تو گرامی بود به ناز آید

Let your presence light up Sa'di's eyes

Anyone passing by the lovers' lane
Will try to return to reason in vain.
The bird in the claws of an eagle
Will never see her nest again.
Your eyebrow is like an altar
That would call an infidel to prayer.
How exalted and happy must be
He who has you each moment to see.
I won't be upset at your bitter words
Sweet as they are from a mouth like yours.
Come and read the sadness off my yellow face
For if I tell the story it will take years.
I am shouting of heart- and mourning of head-ache
These are not just words that come from the mouth.
Put your feet not on dust but on Sa'di's eyes
Anyone as good as you must be a coquette and enticing.[31]

من توبه شکستم
گر خلق بگویند که من عاشق و مستم
آوازه درست است که من توبه شکستم
گر دشمنم ایذا کند و دوست ملامت
من فارغم از هر چه بگویند که هستم
ای نفس که مطلوب تو ناموس و ریا بود
از بند تو برخاستم و خوش بنشستم
از روی نگارین تو بیزارم اگر من
تا روی تو دیدم به دگر کس نگرستم
زین پیش بر آمیختمی با همه مردم
تا یار بدیدم در اغیار ببستم
ای ساقی از آن پیش که مستم کنی از می
من خود ز نظر در قد و بالای تو مستم
شبها گذرد بر من از اندیشه رویت
تا روز نه من خفته نه همسایه ز دستم
حیف است سخن گفتن با هر کس از آن لب
دشنام به من ده که درودت بفرستم
دیریست که سعدی به دل از عشق تو می گفت
این بت نه عجب باشد اگر من بپرستم
بند همه غم های جهان بر دل من بود
در بند تو افتادم و از جمله برستم

I've broken my vows

Let the people say I am drunk and in love
It's true I have broken all my vows
Let enemies hurt and friends scold me
I am totally untouched by whatever they told me.
My ego demanded honour and hypocrisy
I liberated myself from it and now I am free
Having seen your face I'd be damned
If I set my eyes on any other friend.
I used to mix and socialise with many
With you, I would not want to see any
I am drunk by looking at your figure, O Saqi
Long before you serve your wine to me.
All night I remain awake thinking of you
So neither I nor the neighbours rest because of you
Please do not talk to anyone else with those lips.
Swear at me, instead, and I'll respond with praise
Long ago your love made Sa'di tell his heart
That no wonder he must worship this icon.
My heart was bound by the fetters of universal sadness
I fell into the fetters of your love and was liberated from it.[32]

نام سعدی به عشق بازی رفت
نه خود اندر زمین نظیر تو نیست
که قمر چون رخ منیر تو نیست
ندهم دل به قد و قامت سرو
که چو بالای دلپذیر تو نیست
در همه شهر ای کمان ابرو
کس ندانم که صید تیر تو نیست
دل مردم دگر کسی نبرد
که دلی نیست کان اسیر تو نیست
گر بگیری نظیر من چه کنم
که مرا در جهان نظیر تو نیست
ظاهر آنست کان دل چو حدید
در خور صدر چون حریر تو نیست
همه عالم به عشق بازی رفت
نام سعدی، که در ضمیر تو نیست

Sa'di's name stood for loving

It's not just that no-one resembles you
The moon itself lacks your shining face
I will not adore the figure of the cypress tree
Since as well-proportioned as yours it cannot be.
Your eyebrow is such a perfect bow
That no-one in town can escape its arrow
No heart will be captured by anyone but you
As there is no heart that is not captive to you.
I cannot do a thing if you choose one like me
Since I know not in the world one like thee
On reflection you'll know that your heart of steel
Does not at all suit your breasts of silk.
Everywhere Sa'di's name stood for love
Except that his name is not in the beloved's mind.[33]

طواف کعبه
ای که رحمت می نیاید بر منت
آفرین بر جان و رحمت بر تنت
قامتت گویم که دلبند است و خوب
یا سخن یا آمدن یا رفتنت
شرمش از روی تو باید آفتاب
کاندر آید بامداد از روزنت
حسن اندامت نمی گویم به شرح
خود حکایت می کند پیراهنت
ای که سر تا پایت از گل خرمن است
رحمتی کن بر گدای خرمنت
ماهرویا مهربانی پیشه کن
سیرتی چون صورت مستحسنت
ای جمال کعبه رویی باز کن
تا طوافی می کنم پیرامنت
دست گیر این چند روزم در حیات
تا نگیرم در قیامت دامنت
عزم دارم کز دلت بیرون کنم
و اندرون جان بسازم مسکنت
درد دل با سنگدل گفتن چه سود
باد سردی می دمم در آهنت
گفتم از جورت بریزم خون خویش
گفت خون خویشتن در گردنت
گفتم آتش در زنم آفاق را
گفت سعدی درنگیرد با منت

Site of Ka'ba

You have no pity for me at all
But blessed be your body and soul.
How should I praise your figure
Your movements or speech of sugar.
Of your face ashamed must be the sun
When through the window it comes on.
I shall not elaborate on your body
Your garment itself tells its story.
You who are a harvest of flowers
Give some to your flower's beggar.
O ravishing beauty try to be as kind
As your moral beauty would demand.
O site of Ka'ba show me a sign
So I can turn around you like a divine.
Take my hand in the few days of this world
So I will not hold you to God in the next world.
Out of my heart I intend to throw you whole
And give you an abode within my soul.
No use complaining to a heart of stone
Which is just like blowing cold air at iron.
I told her I would spill my blood
She said it would be on your own head.
I shall set fire to the horizons, I said
Sa'di I will not catch fire, she said.[34]

عشق در بهار
درخت غنچه برآورد و بلبلان مستند
جهان جوان شد و یاران به عیش بنشستند
حریف مجلس ما خود همیشه دل می برد
علی الخصوص که پیرایه ای بر او بستند
کسان که در رمضان چنگ می شکستندی
نسیم گل بشنیدند و توبه بشکستند
بساط سبزه لگدکوب شد به پای نشاط
ز بس که عارف و عامی به رقص برجستند
دو دوست قدر شناسند عهد صحبت را
که مدتی ببریدند و باز پیوستند
به در نمی رود از خانقه یکی هشیار
که پیش شحنه بگوید که صوفیان مستند
یکی درخت گل اندر فضای خلوت ماست
که سروهای چمن پیش قامتش پستند
اگر جهان همه دشمن شود، به دولت دوست
خبر ندارم از ایشان که در جهان هستند
مثال راکب دریاست حال کشته عشق
که ترک بار بگفتند و خویشتن رستند
به سرو گفت کسی میوه ای نمی آری
جواب داد که آزادگان تهی دستند
به راه عقل برفتند سعدیا بسیار
که ره به عالم دیوانگان ندانستند

Love in spring

Trees are in bloom, nightingales drunk
The world has turned young, friends in joyful truck.
Full of charm always was our drinking partner
Now adorned, she is more charming than ever.
Those who during Ramadan broke the harp
Heard the flower breathe and broke their fast.
The lawn has been beaten down delightfully
By the mystics and non-mystics dancing joyously.
Two friends will appreciate friendship's fire
Who parted for a while then returned in full desire.
No sober person leaves the Sufis' abode [*khaneqah*]
To tell the police that the Sufis are inebriate.
In our quaint garden there is a floral tree
More balanced in figure than the cypress tree.
If the whole world becomes my enemy, I swear
By my beloved that of none other I will care.
He whom love has killed looks like seafarers
Who dropped their cargo and survived themselves.
The cypress tree was asked why it bore no fruit
The free, it replied, are empty in hand and foot.
Many, O Sa'di, took the road to Rationality
Because they knew not the path of Insanity.[35]

من حیرانم
آن نه روی است که من وصف جمالش دانم
این حدیث از دگری پرس که من حیرانم
همه بینند، نه این صنع که من می بینم
همه خوانند، نه این نقش که من می خوانم
آن عجب نیست که سر گشته بود طالب دوست
عجب این است که من واصل و سرگردانم
سرو در باغ نشانند و ترا بر سر و چشم
گر اجازت دهی ای سرو روان بنشانم
عشق من بر گل رخسار تو امروزی نیست
دیر سالیست که من بلبل این بستانم
به سرت کز سر پیمان محبت نروم
گر بفرمائی رفتن به سر پیکانم
باش تا جان برود در طلب جانانم
که به کاری به از این باز نیاید جانم
هر نصیحت که کنی بشنوم ای یار عزیز
صبرم از دوست مفرمای که من نتوانم
عجب از طبع هوسناک منت می آید
من خود از مردم بی طبع عجب می مانم
گفته بودی: که بود در همه عالم سعدی؟
من به خود هیچ نیم هر چه تو گویی آنم
گر به تشریف قبولم بنوازی ملکم
ور به تازانه قهرم بزنی شیطانم

I am wonderstruck

That is not a face whose beauty I can express
Let someone else do it as I am astounded.
They all see, but that is not the art which *I* see
They all read, but that is not the passage which *I* read.
It is no wonder that her seekers are wondering
It is a wonder that I am with her and still wondering.
They plant the cypress tree in the orchard
Moving cypress, let me put you on my eye and on my head!
Loving the flower of your face is not new
It's years that I have sung in this garden like a nightingale.
By your head I will never break my pledge to you
Even if you order me to sacrifice my life for you.
Let me lose my life for the sake of the one I love
Since nothing better than that would bring me back to life.
Dearest love I will listen to any of your advice
Except if you tell me to be patient with your loss.
You wonder about my eagerly passionate nature
Whereas I wonder at those who lack such nature.
You had said 'Who in the world is Sa'di?'
I am nothing and no-one, except what you call me.
If you do me the honour of having me I am an angel
And if you violently reject me I am Satan.[36]

ماه و نهال
ای باغ حسن چون تو نهالی نیافته
رخساره زمین چو تو خالی نیافته
تابنده‌تر ز روی تو ماهی ندیده چرخ
خوشتر ز ابروی تو هلالی نیافته
بر دور عارض تو نظر کرده آفتاب
خود را لطافتی و جمالی نیافته
چرخ مشعبد از رخ تو دلفریب‌تر
در زیر هفت پرده خیالی نیافته
خود را به زیر چنگل شاهین عشق تو
عنقای صبر من پر و بالی نیافته
تا کی ز درد عشق تو نالد روان من
روزی به لطف از تو مثالی نیافته
افتاده در زبان خلایق حدیث من
با تو به یک حدیث مجالی نیافته
زایل شود هر آنچه بکلی کمال یافت
عمرم زوال یافت کمالی نیافته
گلبرگ عیش من به چه امید بشکفد؟
از بوستان وصل شمالی نیافته
سعدی هزار جامه به روزی قبا کند
یک مهربانی از تو به سالی نیافته

Moon-face sapling

The garden of beauty has not moulded a shoot like you
The face of the earth is void of a mole like you.
A brighter moon the wheel of sky has not seen
A crescent thinner than your eyebrow has not been.
The sun has looked around your face
And has failed to make for her beauty a case.
In its seven layers the wily wheel is yet to find
One more bewitching than your charming smile.
The hawk of my patience is yet to fly
Its wings in the claws of the condor of your love.
How long should my soul moan of the pain of your love
Without even once seeing an example of your kindness.
I have become the talk of the town among the crowd
And yet have not received from you one word.
Whoever rises to his peak tends to decline
I am declining and not having reached the top line.
In what hope should the bud of my life open
Having not had a breeze from the orchard of union.
Sa'di tears down a thousand garments in grief every day
Without receiving one word of kindness from you in a year.[37]

کاروان عالم اسرار
هر گه که بر من آن بت عیار بگذرد
صد کاروان عالم اسرار بگذرد
مست شراب و خواب و جوانی و شاهدی
هر لحظه پیش مردم هشیار بگذرد
هر که بگذرد بکشد دوستان خویش
وین دوست منتظر که دگر بار بگذرد
گفتم به گوشه ای بنشینم چو عاقلان
دیوانه ام کند چو پریوار بگذرد
گفتم دری ز خلق ببندم به روی خویش
دردیست در دلم که ز دیوار بگذرد
بازار حسن جمله خوبان شکسته ای
ره نیست کز تو هیچ خریدار بگذرد
غایب مشو که عمر گرانمایه ضایع است
الا دمی که در نظر یار بگذرد
آسایش است رنج کشیدن به بوی آنک
روزی طبیب بر سر بیمار بگذرد
ترسم که مست و عاشق و بیدل شود چو ما
گر محتسب به خانه خمار بگذرد
سعدی به خویشتن نتوان رفت سوی دوست
کانجا طریق نیست که اغیار بگذرد

Trails of mystery

Each time that wayward idol passes by me
A hundred trails of mystery mystify me.
Drunk with wine, sleep, youthfulness and beauty
That is how each time she passes by the sober society.
Each time she passes she kills her friends
Yet the friends long for her passing again.
I thought I'd sit like a man of reason in a corner
But that angel turns me mad when she turns the corner.
I thought I'd turn into a recluse and shut out the world
But the pain of love even pierces through the wall.
You have broken the market of all that is beautiful
There is no room left for buyers to pass at all.
Do not withdraw as the sweet life is worthless
Except with the beloved, the moment of bliss.
There is comfort in suffering when there is hope
That the doctor would one day manage.
Perhaps if the morality policeman passes by the tavern
He would also turn drunk, loving and unconscious.
Sa'di one cannot go to the beloved by oneself
There is no road there for strangers to pass without help.[38]

DESCRIPTIONS
of the BELOVED

...برهنه اندامت
سرو قدی میان انجمنی
به که هفتاد سرو در چمنی
چهل باشد فراق صحبت دوست
بتماشای لاله و سمنی
ای که هرگز ندیده ای به جمال
جز در آیینه مثل خویشتنی
تو که همتای خویشتن بینی
لاجرم ننگری به مثل منی
در دهانت سخن نمی گویم
که نگنجد در آن دهن سخنی
بدنت در میان پیرهنت
همچو روحیست رفته در بدنی
وانکه بیند برهنه اندامت
گوید این پر گل است پیرهنی
با وجودت خطا بود که نظر
به ختایی کنند یا ختنی
باد اگر در من اوفتد ببرد
که نماندست زیر جامه تنی
چاره بیچارگی بود سعدی
چون ندانند چاره ای و فنی

...*Your naked body*

One with an image of the cypress tree
Is better than many real cypress trees
How can one leave the beloved's side
And go and see jasmine and tulip aside?
Except in the mirror, you will never have seen
As beautiful as yourself a scene
Seeing just your own reflection
How could you give the likes of me attention?
The size of your mouth I will not mention
It cannot hold even a word by intention
Wrapped in its garment, your body
Is just like a soul inside a body.
And he who would see you naked
Would say it is just a flower bed
With you in sight it will be a mistake
To behold other beauties instead.
If the wind comes it will blow me away
For I am just a raiment with no body
The remedy, O Sa'di, is despair
When there is no remedy or repair.[39]

شکر و عسل
جان و تنم ای دوست فدای تن و جانت
مویی نفروشم به همه ملک جهانت
شیرین تر از این لب نشنیدم که سخن گفت
تو خود شکری یا عسل است آب دهانت؟
یک روز عنایت کن و تیری به من انداز
باشد که تفرج بکنم دست و کمانت
گر راه بگردانی و گر روی بپوشی
من می نگرم گوشه چشم نگرانت
بر سرو نباشد رخ چون ماه منیرت
بر ماه نباشد قد چون سرو روانت
آخر چه بلایی تو که در وصف نیایی
بسیار بگفتیم و نکردیم بیانت
هر کس که ملامت کند از عشق تو ما را
معذور بدارند چو بینند عیانت
حیف است چنین روی نگارین که بپوشی
سودی به مساکین رسد آخر چه زیانت
باز آی که در دیده بماندست خیالت
بنشین که به خاطر بنشستست نشانت
بسیار نباشد دلی از دست بدادن
از جان رمقی دارم و هم برخی جانت
دشنام کرم کردی و گفتی و شنیدم
خرم تن سعدی که برآمد به زبانت

Sugar and honey

Let my body and soul be a sacrifice to you beloved
I will not exchange a hair of yours for the whole world
Sweeter than these lips I have not heard anyone speak
Speak, are you sugar itself or your mouth honey?
One day be kind and at me throw a dart
Luckily your hand and dart will be right
Whether you turn back or cover your face
I will see the corner of your eye in the chase.
The cypress tree lacks your moonlit face
What calamity, after all, are you?
Hard as I tried I was unable to describe you
The moon has not your cypress-tree grace.
Whoever blames me for loving you
Will take back the blame when seeing you
It is wasteful that you cover this picture of a face
Open, it profits the needy and costs you not a pittance.
Come back, for in my eyes has remained your sight
Sit down, since your face has settled in my mind
It's not all that much losing my heart
I've just one breath left which to you I'll sacrifice.
Gracefully you swore at me; it made my fame
Happy is Sa'di now that you mention his name.[40]

معجز و کرامت
این که تو داری قیامت است نه قامت
وین نه تبسم که معجز است و کرامت
هر که تماشای روی چون قمرت کرد
سینه سپر کرد پیش تیر ملامت
هر شب و روزی که بی تو می رود از عمر
بر نفسی می رود هزار ندامت
عمر نبود آنچه غافل از تو نشستم
باقی عمر ایستاده ام به غرامت
سرو خرامان چو قد معتدلت نیست
آن همه وصفش که می کنند به قامت
چشم مسافر که بر جمال تو افتاد
عزم رحیلش بدل شود به اقامت
اهل فریقین در تو خیره بمانند
گر بروی در حسابگاه قیامت
این همه سختی و نامرادی سعدی
چون تو پسندی سعادت است و سلامت

Miracle and grace

Your figure is beyond praise
Your smile nothing but miracle and grace
Whoever saw your moon-shaped face
Loved it and was ready to be blamed.
Each day and night that I am without you
My every word is filled with remorse
The time I spent without you I don't call life
All my life I have tried to make up for this loss.
The cypress tree, praised so much for its stature,
Pales before your well-proportioned figure
If a traveller sets his eye on you
He will change his mind and not go.
If you rise on the Day of Resurrection
All parties will be dazzled by your reflection.
If you like all that Sa'di suffers
Then the suffering counts as health and happiness.[41]

چه شیرین دهن است آن

در وصف نیاید که چه شیرین دهن است آن
این است که دور از لب و دندان من است آن
عارض نتوان گفت که دور قمر است آن
بالا نتوان خواند که سرو چمن است آن
در سرو رسیدست ولیکن به حقیقت
از سرو گذشتست که سیمین بدن است آن
هرگز نبود جسم بدین حسن و لطافت
گویی همه روح است که در پیرهن است آن
خال است بر آن صفحه سیمین بناگوش
یا نقطه ای از غالیه بر یاسمن است آن؟
فی الجمله قیامت تویی امروز در آفاق
در چشم تو پیداست که باب فتن است آن
گفتم که دل از چنبر زلفت برهانم
ترسم نرهانم که شکن بر شکن است آن
هر کس که به جان آرزوی وصل تو دارد
دشوار بر آید که محقر ثمن است آن
گر خسته دلی نعره زند بر سر کویی
عیبش نتوان گفت که بی خویشتن است آن
نزدیک من آن است که هر جور و خطایی
کز صاحب وجه حسن آید حسن است آن
سعدی سر سودای تو دارد نه سر خویش
هر جامه که عیار بپوشد کفن است آن

The sweetness of her mouth

The sweetness of her mouth is divine
No wonder that it is far from mine
Don't call it a face, it's a full moon
Don't call it a figure, it's a cypress tree.
But in fact she has surpassed the cypress tree
For her body is made of silver
Never will you find a body as delicate as this
It's as if her soul alone fills her dress.
Is it a mole on that silvery ear
Or a piece of musk on a jasmine flower?
In short you are the chaos in the world today
And one can see the riot in your eye.
I tried to liberate my heart from the curl of your hair
But I may not succeed as it is full of curls
Wishing to sacrifice one's life to have you
Is difficult to fulfil for the price is small.
If a sad lover shouts in your neighbourhood
He cannot be blamed for he is not in control
I believe that any offence or error
Committed by a beauty is fine.
Sa'di only thinks of you not of himself
Any raiment worn by a libertine is a shroud.[42]

لعلی چو لب شکر فشانت

من چون تو به دلبری ندیدم
گلبرگ چنین طری ندیدم
مانند تو آدمی در آفاق
ممکن نبود، پری ندیدم
وین بوالعجبی و چشم بندی
در صنعت سامری ندیدم
با روی تو ماه آسمان را
امکان برابری ندیدم
لعلی چو لب شکر فشانت
در کلبه جوهری ندیدم
چون در دو رسته دهانت
نظم سخن دری ندیدم
مه را که خرد که من به کرات
مه دیدم و مشتری ندیدم
وین پرده راز پارسایان
چندان که تو می دری ندیدم
دیدم همه دلبران آفاق
چون تو به دلاوری ندیدم
جوری که تو می کنی در اسلام
در ملت کافری ندیدم
سعدی غم عشق خوبرویان
چندان که تو می خوری ندیدم
دیدم همه صوفیان آفاق
مثل تو قلندری ندیدم

The ruby of your lips

None as enticing as you have I come across
No flower as fresh as you have I crossed
It's impossible to find humans, not even fairies,
Like you anywhere, even on all the horizons.
Nor have I seen the like of your magical art
In the magic performed by the golden calf
Nor can the moon shining in blue sky
Compete with your radiant appearance.
Nor have I seen a ruby like your sweet lips
Among the rubies in a jeweller's ruby bag
And like the two rows of pearls in your mouth
I have not even found the pearls of the Persian tongue.
Who would buy the moon since many a time
I saw the moon without a customer in line?
Nor have I seen anyone like you
Revealing the secrets of your pious lovers.
I saw all the sweethearts everywhere
But did not find one as audacious as you
And the cruelty you commit in Islamic lands
I have not seen committed in the lands of the infidels.
Sa'di, I have seen no-one who as much as you
Suffers from the love of pretty-faced people
I did see all the Sufis of the world
But not one as libertine as you.[43]

لب شیرین شکربار
کس ندانم که در این شهر گرفتار تو نیست
هیچ بازار چنین گرم که بازار تو نیست
سرو زیبا و به زیبایی بالای تو نه
شهد شیرین و به شیرینی گفتار تو نیست
خود که باشد که ترا بیند و عاشق نشود
مگرش هیچ نباشد که خریدار تو نیست
کس ندیدست ترا یک نفس اندر همه عمر
که همه عمر دعاگوی و هوادار تو نیست
آدمی نیست مگر کالبدی بی جان است
آنکه گوید که مرا میل به دیدار تو نیست
ای که شمشیر جفا بر سر ما آخته ای
صلح کردیم که ما را سر پیکار تو نیست
جور تلخ است ولیکن چه کنم گر نبرم
چون گریز از لب شیرین شکر بار تو نیست
من سری دارم و در پای تو خواهم بازید
خجل از ننگ بضاعت که سزاوار تو نیست
به جمال تو که دیدار ز من باز نگیر
که مرا طاقت نادیدن دیدار تو نیست
سعدیا گر نتوانی که کم خود گیری
سر خود گیر که صاحب‌نظری کار تو نیست

Sweet sugary lips

I know no-one who is not bewitched by you
No bazaar is as busy as the bazaar of loving you.
The cypress tree is beautiful but not like your figure
Honey is sweet but not as sweet as your speech.
No-one who sees you would not fall in love with you
He who seeks you not must have nothing to offer you.
There is no-one who has seen you for one breath
Who will not want you and pray for you until death.
It is not a human, only a lifeless corpse perhaps
Who would say he does not long to set eyes on you.
You have drawn the dagger of unkindness against me
Peace! Because I have no intention of fighting thee.
Suffering is hard but I am prepared to put up with it
Since there is no choice of ignoring your sweet sugary lips.
I have a head and am ready to lose it at your feet
I am only embarrassed that they are not worthy of it.
By your beauty do not stop me from seeing you
Since I cannot possibly bear not seeing you.
If you cannot keep yourself and your own, Sa'di
Then give up since you lack the art of loving.[44]

با تو صورت دیوار در نمی گنجد
حدیث عشق به طومار در نمی گنجد
بیان دوست به گفتار در نمی گنجد
سماع انس که دیوانگان از آن مستند
به سمع مردم هشیار در نمی گنجد
میسرت نشود عاشقی و مستوری
ورع به خانه خمار در نمی گنجد
چنان فراخ نشستست یار در دل تنگ
که بیش زحمت اغیار در نمی گنجد
ترا چنان که تویی من صفت ندانم کرد
که عرض جامه به بازار در نمی گیجد
دگر به صورت هیچ آفریده دل ندهم
که با تو صورت دیوار در نمی گنجد
خبر که می دهد امشب رقیب مسکین را
که سگ به زاویه غار در نمی گنجد
چو گل به بار بود همنشین خار بود
چو در کنار بود خار در نمی گنجد
چنان ارادت و شوق است در میان دو دوست
که سعی دشمن خونخوار در نمی گنجد
به چشم دل نظرت می کنم که دیده سر
ز برق شعله دیدار در نمی گنجد
ز دوستان که ترا هست جای سعدی نیست
گدا میان خریدار در نمی گنجد

No portrayal does your face justice

Love is not a story that can be written
The beloved's description cannot be spoken.
The song of friendship which inebriates the mad
Cannot reach the ears of those who are sober.
You won't be able to love and treat it secretly
Just as the tavern is not a place for piety.
She has filled the labyrinths of my heart so well
That no room is left for strangers to intrude.
I cannot tell what in fact you are
How can one take cloths to a merchant clothier?
I will never worship any other person's face
For not even a picture compares with your face.
Who will tell my miserable rival tonight
That he has no hope in a thousand nights?
The flower on the branch sits with thorns
But when it is in your hand it feels warm.
The bond of our friendship is so strong
That the enemy's campaign will not do wrong.
I watch you with my heart's eye since
My head's eye cannot bear the light in your eyes.
You have so many friends that there is no room for Sa'di
What can a poor man do among so many buyers?[45]

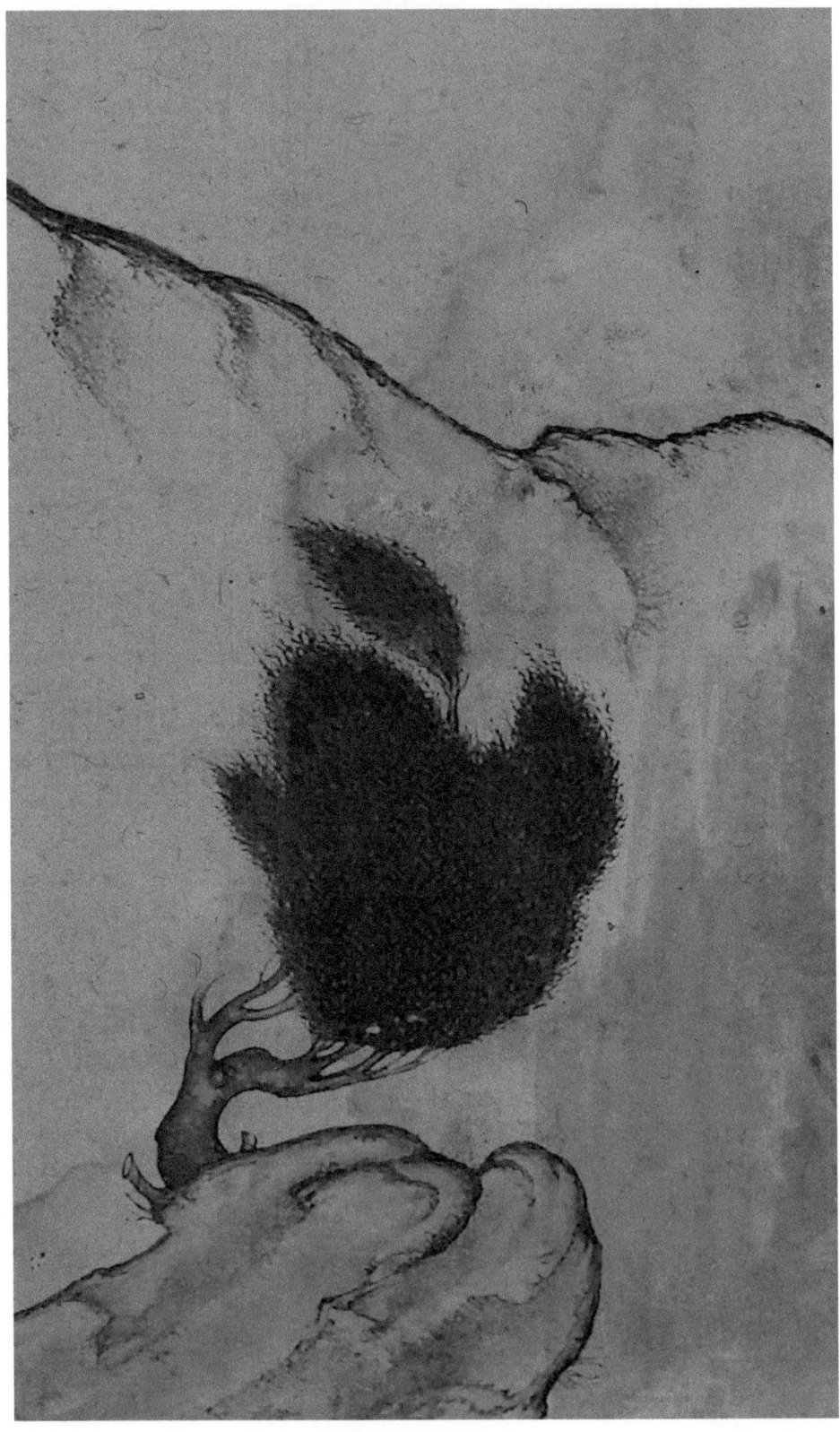

UNION

جهان گلزار می بینم
منم یا رب در این دولت که روی یار می بینم
فراز سرو سیمینش گلی پر بار می بینم؟
مگر طوبی بر آمد در سرابستان جان من
که بر هر شعبه ای مرغی شکرگفتار می بینم؟
مگر دنیا سرآمد کاین چنین آزاد در جنت
می بی درد می نوشم گل بی خار می بینم؟
عجب دارم ز بخت خویش و هر دم در گمان افتم
که مستم، یا بخوابم، یا جمال یار می بینم
زمین بوسیده ام بسیار و خدمت کرده تا اکنون
لب معشوق می بوسم رخ دلدار می بینم.
چه طاعت کرده ام گویی که این پاداش می یابم؟
چه فرمان برده ام گویی که این مقدار می بینم؟
تویی یارا که خواب‌آلوده بر من تاختن کردی
منم یا رب که بخت خود چنین بیدار می بینم؟
چو خلوت در میان آمد نخواهم شمع کاشانه
تمنای بهشتم نیست چون دیدار می بینم
کدامین لاله می بویم که مغزم عنبرآگین شد
چه ریحان دسته بندم چون جهان گلزار می بینم؟
ز گردون نعره می آید که اینت بوالعجب کاری
که سعدی را ز روی دوست برخوردار می بینم

I see flowers everywhere

God, am I so fortunate that I see the beloved's face
Above her silvery figure a flower full of grace?
Did the heavenly tree grow in the garden of my soul
That in every branch I see a bird with a sweet call?
Has the world expired that so freely in paradise
I drink pure wine and see flowers thornless?
I am astonished at my luck and keep wondering
Am I drunk or asleep, or is it the beloved I am seeing?
I have knelt and worshipped her many a time
Now I see her face and kiss her lips all the time.
What good have I done to deserve such a reward?
What service have I performed to be lifted so upward?
Is it you beloved galloping towards me sleepily?
Is it me, O God, being in so much luck so deeply?
Now that we are alone I do not want a candle
Being with her, paradise I do not wish to handle.
What rose did I smell that has perfumed my head?
What flowers should I gather when the world is a flower bed?
I hear a voice saying what a wonderful felicity
That Saʿdi is enjoying the beloved's company.[46]

شور عشق
نه آن شب است که کس در میان ما گنجد
به خاک پایت اگر ذره در هوا گنجد
کلاه ناز و تکبر بنه، کمر بگشای
که چون تو سرو ندیدم که در قبا گنجد
ز من حکایت هجران مپرس در شب وصل
عتاب کیست که در خلوت رضا گنجد؟
مرا شکر منه و گل مریز در مجلس
میان خسرو و شیرین شکر کجا افتد؟
چو شور عشق درآمد قرار عقل نماند
درون مملکتی چون دو پادشا گنجد؟
نماند در سر سعدی ز بانگ رود و سرود
مجال آن که دگر پند پارسا گنجد

Passion for love

No-one can come between us tonight
By the dust I swear not even a particle might.
Stop the coquetry and pride; take off your headdress
Open your cummerbund and let out that cypress.
Stop asking me about the sadness of separation
Now we are together, complaints bring no salvation.
Do not bring me flowers and offer me sugar
Khosrow and Shirin are not in need of sugar.[47]
The passion for love came, reason departed
How can two kings coexist in one kingdom?
Sa'di listened to so much music and song
That left him no time for listening to pious advice.[48]

در آغوش یار
یک امشبی که در آغوش شاهد شکرم
گرم چو عود بر آتش نهند غم نخورم
چو التماس برآمد هلاک باکی نیست
کجاست تیر بلا گو بیا که من سپرم
ببند یک نفس ای آسمان دریچه صبح
بر آفتاب، که امشب خوش است با قمرم
ندانم این شب قدر است یا ستاره روز
تویی برابر من یا خیال در نظرم؟
خوشا هوای گلستان و عشق در بستان
اگرنبودی تشویش بلبل سحرم
بدین دو دیده که امشب ترا همی بینم
دریغ باشد فردا به دیگری نگرم
روان تشنه برآساید از وجود فرات
مرا فرات ز سر برگذشت و تشنه ترم
چو می ندیدمت از شوق بی خبر بودم
کنون که با تو نشستم ز ذوق بی خبرم
سخن بگوی که بیگانه پیش ما کس نیست
بغیر شمع و همین ساعتش زبان ببرم
میان ما بجز این پیرهن نخواهد بود
وگر حجاب شود تا به دامنش بدرم
مگوی، سعدی از این عشق جان نخواهد برد
بگو کجا برم آن جان که از غمت ببرم

In the beloved's embrace

This one night in my beloved's embrace
If they set me on fire it would leave no trace
Once my desire is fulfilled, death brings no fear
I am ready like a shield for the arrow of fate.
O heavens shut the morning's window to the sun
Tonight I am happy with the moon as it shines
Is this the morning star or the Sacred Night?
Is it you in front of me or just your thought?
I wish we could go and sleep out on the lawn
If I did not worry about the nightingale of the dawn
These two eyes with which tonight I see you
It'll be a pity if I set them on another tomorrow.
The soul of the thirsty is soothed by a river
In the river I am drowning and am thirstier
In your absence I did not know delight
Now that I see you in joy I am enchanted.
Speak! There is no stranger except the candle
Whose tongue I will cut off this moment and handle
Nothing would separate us except this garment
And if it comes between us I will tear it apart.
Do not say Sa'di will not survive this love
Tell me how I can shed the sadness of your love.[49]

دیدار با یار
بسم از هواگرفتن که پری نماند و بالی
به کجا روم ز دستت که نمی دهی مجالی
نه ره گریز دارم نه طریق آشنایی
چه غم اوفتاده ای را که تواند احتیالی
چه خوش است در فراقی همه عمر صبر کردن
به امید آنکه روزی به کف اوفتد وصالی
به تو حاصلی ندارد غم روزگار گفتن
که شبی نخفته باشی به درازنای سالی
غم حال دردمندان نه عجب گرت نباشد
که چنین نرفته باشد همه عمر بر تو حالی
سخنی بگوی با من که چنان اسیر عشقم
که به خویشتن ندارم ز وجودت اشتغالی
چه نشینی ای قیامت بنمای سرو قامت
به خلاف سرو بستان که ندارد اعتدالی
که نه امشب آن سماع است که دف خلاص یابد
به طپانچه ای و بربط برهد به گوشمالی
دگر آفتاب رویت منمای آسمان را
که قمر ز شرمساری بشکست چون هلالی
خط مشکبوی و خالت به مناسبت تو گویی
قلم غبار می رفت و فرو چکید خالی
تو هم این نگوی سعدی که نظر گناه باشد
گنه است بر گرفتن نظر از چنین جمالی

Being with the beloved

Enough of taking off, I have no wings left
Where can I take your thought when you are here?
I can neither run away nor be with you
Down and out, I wish I could find a way.
I spent all my life far away from you
It would be good if on the Day of Judgement I see you
It's good to suffer separation all one's life
If there is hope of reunion at least once.
There is no point in speaking to you of pain
Since your night has never been as long as a year
Speak to me for I am so deeply in love
That I have lost myself at your side.
Why sit, rise up and show your fine figure
(Proportioned as it is unlike the cypress tree)
Since this is not a joyful song and dance
That the lyre and the drum will play only once.
Stop showing the sun-shaped face in the firmament
It shames the moon and breaks it into a crescent
Your sweet-smelling *khatt* and mole look as if
The pen of dust was moving and it dropped a drip.
Do not say, Sa'di, that looking [*nazar*] is a sin
To stop looking at such a beauty is a sin.[50]

مبادا که گنجی ببیند فقیر
مرا راحت از زندگی دوش بود
که آن ماهرویم در آغوش بود
چنان مست دیدار و حیران عشق
که دنیا و دینم فراموش بود
نگویم می لعل شیرین گوار
که زهر از کف دست او نوش بود
ندانستم از غایت لطف و حسن
که سیم و سمن یا بر و دوش بود
بدیدار و گفتار جان پرورش
سراپای من دیده و گوش بود
نمی دانم آن شب که چون روز شد
کسی بازداند که باهوش بود
موذن غلط کرد بانگ نماز
مگر همچو من مست و مدهوش بود
بگفتیم و دشمن بدانست و دوست
نماند آن تحمل که سرپوش بود
بخوابش مگر دیده ای سعدیا
زبان درکش امروز کان دوش بود
مبادا که گنجی ببیند فقیر
که نتواند از حرص خاموش بود

Discovery of a treasure

Last night I felt the joy of life
When that beauty was in my arms
So drunk was I by love and her presence
That I had forgotten both life and providence.
I will not call it sweet agreeable ruby wine
Since even poison from her hands was divine
I had not known that beauty could seem
As if it were made of silver and jasmine.
Seeing and talking to her lifted up my soul
I was eyes and ears from head to toe
I know not how this night ended with the day
I might have known if I had not lost consciousness.
The muezzin called for morning prayer too early
Perhaps like me he was drunk and melancholy
We did not have the patience to hide our union
So both friend and enemy learned of what had happened.
Sa'di, you might have seen her in a dream
Say no more today since that was last night
Let no man discover a treasure house
Since he'd be too joyful to hold his tongue.[51]

در آتش چو خلیل

آمدی وه که چه مشتاق و پریشان بودم
تا برفتی ز برم صورت بی جان بودم
نه فراموشی ام از ذکر تو خاموش نشاند
که در اندیشه اوصاف تو حیران بودم
بی تو در دامن گلزار نخفتم یک شب
که نه در بادیه خار مغیلان بودم
زنده می کرد مرا دمبدم امید وصال
ور نه دور از نظرت کشته هجران بودم
به تولای تو در آتش محنت چو خلیل
گویبا در چمن لاله و ریحان بودم
تا مگر یک نفسم بوی تو آرد دم صبح
همه شب منتظر مرغ سحرخوان بودم
سعدی از جور فراقت شب و روز این می گفت
عهد بشکستی و من بر سر پیمان بودم

Engulfed in fire like Abraham

You went and I was a soulless face
You came when I was dishevelled and desirous.
I stopped mentioning you not out of forgetfulness
I was just puzzled about how to sing your praise.
Without you, sleeping in a bed of flowers
Felt as if I were in a desert full of thistles.
What kept me alive was the hope of union
Otherwise I would have been killed by separation.
By your friendship being engulfed in fire like Abraham
It felt as if I were in a lawn full of tulips and sweet basil.
In the hope that I receive your scent once at dawn
All night I was waiting for the dawn-bird to moan.
Suffering from separation Sa'di kept saying
You broke your pledge but I honoured mine.[52]

لکم دینکم و لی دینی
شب است و شاهد و شمع و شراب و شیرینی
غنیمت است چنین شب که دوستان بینی
به شرط آنکه منت بنده وار در خدمت
بایستم، تو خداوند وار بنشینی
میان ما و شما عهد در ازل رفتست
هزار سال بر آید همان نخستینی
چو صبرم از تو میسر نمی شود چه کنم
به خشم رفتم و باز آمدم به مسکینی
به حکم آنکه مرا هیچ دوست چون تو به دست
نیاید و، تو به از من هزار بگزینی
به رنگ و بوی بهار ای فقیر قانع باش
چو باغبان نگذارد که سیب و گل چینی
تفاوتی نکند گر ترش کنی ابرو
هزار تلخ بگویی هنوز شیرینی
لگام بر سر شیران کند صلابت عشق
چنان کشد که شتر را مهار در بینی
ز نیکبختی، سعدیست پای بند غمت
زهی کبوتر مقبل که صید شاهینی
مرا شکیب نمی باشد ای مسلمانان
ز روی خوب، لکم دینکم و لی دینی

Your faith is yours and mine is mine

There is beauty, candlelight, wine and sweets this night
Cherish such a night when you see those you love
On the condition that I stand as your servant
And you sit down like my lord and master.
You and I made our pledge at the dawn of creation
Even if a thousand years pass you'll still be my choice.
I cannot bear being separated from you
So I went in anger and returned humble
Because I will never have a beloved like you
While you can choose a thousand better than me.
Poor man be content with the spring's colours and scents
When the gardener does not let you pick apples and flowers
It will make no difference, my love, if you frown
Bitter words you may utter but you are still sweet.
Lions would be pulled by the strength of love
And as hard it would be as the rein pulls a camel
Sa'di is fortunate to suffer sadness for you
Like a fortunate pigeon in the claws of an eagle.
I have no patience with good looks O Muslims
Your faith is yours and mine is mine.[53]

شب وصل
یا رب شب دوشین چه مبارک سحری بود
کو را به سر کشته هجران گذری بود
آن دوست که ما را به ارادت نظری داشت
با ما مگر او را به عنایت نظری بود
من بعد شکایت نکنم تلخی هجران
کان میوه که از صبر برآمد شکری بود
رویی نتوان گفت که حسنش به چه ماند
گویی که در آن نیم شب از روز دری بود
گویم قمری بود کس از من نپسندد:
باغی که به هر شاخ درختش قمری بود
آن دم که خبر بودم از او تا تو نگویی
کز خویشتن و هر که جهانم خبری بود
در عالم وصفش به جهانی برسیدم
کاندر نظرم هر دو جهان مختصری بود
من بودم و او، نی، قلم اندر سر من کش
با او نتوان گفت وجود دگری بود
با غمزه خوبان که چو شمشیر کشیدست
در صبر بدیدم که نه محکم سپری بود
سعدی نتوانی که دگر دیده بدوزی
کان دل بربودند که صبرش قدری بود

Night of union

God what a blessèd dawn was last night's union
As she was visiting me dead from separation.
It showed that the beloved I much adore
Also cares for the one whom she adores.
Henceforth I will not moan about separation
Since the fruit of patience was sensation.
It is impossible to say what she looked like
It was as if she and the sun were shining alike.
It would be wrong to say that she was the moon
More a garden with trees adorned by moons.
Having her with me, you should not imagine
That I was aware of anyone else or of me.
While praising her I got as far as a world
Beside which the world was just a little abode.
There was she and me – no, strike the word 'me'
For with her there can be none other than she.
With the beloved's coquetry – a drawn sword –
The shield of patience will never work.
No point in longing, Sa'di, any more
Being robbed of the heart that could endure.[54]

پستان یار
امشب مگر به وقت نمی خواند این خروس
عشاق بس نکرده هنوز از کنار و بوس
پستان یار در خم گیسوی تابدار
چون گوی عاج در خم چوگان آبنوس
یک شب که یار فتنه خفتست زینهار
بیدار باش تا نرود عمر بر فسوس
تا نشنوی ز مسجد آدینه بانگ صبح
یا از در سرای اتابک غریو کوس
لب بر لبی چو چشم خروس، ابلهی بود
برداشتن به گفته بیهوده خروس

The beloved's breast

Does the cock not crow in time, tonight?
Lovers have not yet stopped kissing and delight.
The beloved's breast engulfed in her curly hair
Is like a ball of ivory hit by a black polo mallet.
This night that the beloved is no longer seditious
Try to be awake so your life is not passed useless.
So that the muezzin does not remind you of the dawn
Nor do you hear the morning drums from the king's lawn.
Mouth stuck on mouth like the eye of the cock
It would be folly to stop by the crow of the cock.[55]

گدا و پادشاه
من اگر نظر حرام است بسی گناه دارم
چه کنم نمی توانم که نظر نگاه دارم
ستم از کسیست بر من که ضرورت است بردن
نه قرار زخم خوردن نه مجال آه دارم
نه فراغت نشستن نه شکیب رخت بستن
نه مقام ایستادن نه گریزگاه دارم
نه اگر همی نشینم نظری کند به رحمت
نه اگر همی گریزم دگری پناه دارم
بسم از قبول عامی و صلاح نیکنامی
چو به ترک سر بگفتم چه غم از کلاه دارم
تن من فدای جانت، سر بنده و آستانت
چه مرا به از گدائی چو تو پادشاه دارم
چو ترا بدین نکوئی قدم صلاح باشد
نه مروت است اگر من نظر تباه دارم
چه شبیست یا رب امشب که ستاره ای برآمد
که دگر نه عشق خورشید و نه مهر ماه دارم
مکنید دردمندان گله از شب جدائی
که من این صباح روشن ز شب سیاه دارم
که نه روی خوب دیدن گنه است پیش سعدی
تو گمان نیک بردی که من این گناه دارم

Beggar and lord

If throwing an erotic look is sinful, I am immersed in sin
I have no choice and cannot withhold my look and not sin
She who makes me suffer I have no choice but to obey
Neither can I bear being hurt, nor can I complain.
I have not permission to sit, nor the patience to go
Nor a place to stand, nor anywhere to turn to
Nor if I sit would she throw me a kind look
Nor if I run off is there another to look for.
Enough of general approval and good address
Having delivered the head why worry about the headdress
May my body be a sacrifice to your soul,
    my head on your threshold
What better than being a beggar when I have you as lord?
As pretty as you are, you are good too
It will not be fair if less than that I show
God, what a night is it that with this star in my arms
I no longer love the sun nor desire the moon and stars.
Sufferers stop complaining about the night of separation
Because I have this bright morning
    after a dark night's deliberation
Sa'di does not believe seeing a beautiful face is a sin
Although you thought that he had certainly sinned.[56]

اکسیر عشق
از در درآمدی و من از خود بدر شدم
گفتی کز این جهان به جهان دگر شدم
گوشم به راه تا که خبر می‌دهد ز دوست
صاحب خبر بیامد و من بی خبر شدم
چون شبنم اوفتاده بدم پیش آفتاب
مهرم به جان رسید و به عیوق بر شدم
گفتم ببینمش مگرم درد اشتیاق
ساکن شود، بدیدم و مشتاق‌تر شدم
دستم نداد قوت رفتن به پیش یار
چندی به پای رفتم و چندی به سر شدم
تا رفتنش ببینم و گفتنش بشنوم
از پای تا به سر همه سمع و بصر شدم
من چشم از او چگونه توانم نگاه‌داشت
کاول نظر به دیدن او دیده ور شدم
بیزارم از وفای تو یک روز و یک زمان
مجموع اگر نشستم و خرسند اگر شدم
او را خود التفات نبودش به صید من
من خویشتن اسیر کمند نظر شدم
گویند روی سرخ تو سعدی چه زرد کرد
اکسیر عشق بر مسم افتاد و زر شدم

Alchemy of love

You stepped into my life and I lost control
As if I had moved from this to the other world
My ears ready to receive the news of the friend
The news arrived and I lost news of myself.
Like dew I lay on my face below the sun
Love filled my soul and I rose up to the sky
I thought when I see her the pain of desire will be relieved
I saw her and my desire massively increased.
I did not have the strength to try to reach my friend
Now I walked on my feet and now I walked on my head
To see her move and hear her speak
I became eyes and ears from head to toe.
How can I ever cease to sit and watch her?
I learned seeing after all by opening my eyes to her
I would be inconstant if only for a time
I sat relaxed and happy without you sublime.
It was not she who aimed to hunt me down
I myself fell into her lasso when I saw her run
They ask Sa'di what turned your face yellow
It was the alchemy of love which turned me into gold.[57]

وصال با دوست
مبارک تر شب و خرم ترین روز
به استقبالم آمد بخت پیروز
دهل زن گو دو نوبت زن بشارت
که دوشم قدر بود امروز نوروز
مه است این یا ملک یا آدمیزاد
پری یا آفتاب عالم افروز
ندانستی که ضدان در کمین اند
نکو کردی علی رغم بد آموز
مرا با دوست ای دشمن وصال است
تو را گر دل نخواهد دیده بردوز
شبان دانم که از درد جدائی
نیاسودم ز فریاد جهانسوز
گر آن شب های با وحشت نمی بود
نمی دانست سعدی قدر امروز

In union with my lover

The most blissful night and auspicious day
Were victory's meeting two paces away.
Verily twice must I have song and dance
Once for today's bliss one for last night's.
Is my lover moon, human or angel
Fairy is she or the light of sun?
You did not know the knaves were looking
Yet did the right thing despite their cooking.
Tell the enemy I am in union with my love
And he can go hang from gallows above.
I remember the nights of separation
And the pain of burning sensation.
If Sa'di had not suffered those nights of terror
His day wouldn't have been a shining mirror.[58]

SEPARATION

شب تنهایی
سر آن ندارد امشب که برآید آفتابی
چه خیال ها گذر کرد و گذر نکرد خوابی
به چه دیر ماندی ای صبح که جان من برآمد
بزه کردی و نکردند موذنان ثوابی
نفس خروس بگرفت که نوبتی بخواند
همه بلبلان بمردند و نماند جز غرابی
نفحات صبح دانی ز چه روی دوست دارم
که به روی یار ماند که برافکند نقابی
سرم از خدای خواهد که به پایش اندر افتد
که در آب مرده بهتر که در آرزوی آبی
دل من نه مرد آن است که با غمش برآید
مگسی کجا تواند که برافکند عقابی
نه چنان گناهکارم که به دشمنم سپاری
تو به دست خویش فرمای اگرم کنی عذابی
دل همچو سنگت ای دوست به آب چشم سعدی
عجب است اگر نگردد که بگردد آسیابی
برو ای گدای مسکین و دری دگر طلب کن
که هزار بار گفتی و نیامدت جوابی

A night of loneliness

The sun does not deign to rise upon this night
What thoughts traversed the mind and no sleep in sight.
Why are you so late a morning that I am about to fall
You sinned and the muezzins failed to make their call.
The cock is choking just to try to crow one time
All the nightingales died and only the ravens survived.
Do you know why I love the morning breeze?
It feels as if the beloved's veil has been eased.
My head begs of God to fall down to her feet
Since it is better to die in water than of thirst.
My heart cannot bear the sadness of her love
Just as a bird cannot resist the power of a hawk.
I am not so guilty as to be handed to my enemy
Do it by your own hands if you wish to torture me.
Sa'di's tears alas do not turn your heart of stone
Whereas a mill can turn by the water of my eye alone.
Go off miserable beggar and find another door to solicit
Here you begged a thousand times and got no reply for it.[59]

تحمل نکنم بار جدایی
من ندانستم از اول که تو بی مهر و وفایی
عهد نابستن از آن به که ببندی و نپایی
دوستان عیب کنندم که چرا دل به تو دادم
باید اول به تو گفتن که چنین خوب چرایی
ای که گفتی مرو اندر پی خوبان زمانه
ما کجاییم در این بحر تفکر تو کجایی
آن نه خال است و زنخدان و سر زلف پریشان
که دل اهل نظر برد که سرّیست خدایی
پرده بردار که بیگانه خود آن روی نبیند
تو بزرگی و در آیینه کوچک ننمایی
حلقه بر در نتوانم زدن از بیم رقیبان
این توانم که بیایم به محلت به گدایی
عشق و درویشی و انگشت نمایی و ملامت
همه سهل است تحمل نکنم بار جدایی
روز صحرا و سماع است و لب جوی و تماشا
در همه شهر دلی نیست که دیگر برُبایی
گفته بودم که بیایی غم دل با تو بگویم
چه بگویم که غم از دل برود چون تو بیایی
شمع را باید از این خانه برون بردن و کشتن
تا به همسایه نگوید که تو در خانه مایی
سعدی آن نیست که هرگز ز کمندت بگریزد
که بدانست که در بند تو بهتر که رهایی
خلق گویند برو دل به هوای دگری ده
نکنم خاصه در ایام اتابک دو هوایی

Separation is unbearable sorrow
Little did I know that constancy and kindness you lack
It's better not to make a pledge than to break it.
Friends blame me for giving my heart to you
They should tell you first why so unforgettable are you.
He who warns me not to love the beauties of our time
His world and mine are worlds apart.
That is not just a mole, a chin, dishevelled hair
It's ravished everyone's heart as it is God's secret.
Drop the veil for the stranger will not see your face
You are too great to be reflected in a small mirror case.
For fear of rivals I cannot knock at your door
Only disguised as a beggar can I come to your abode.
Love, poverty, being caught and scolded
It'll all come easy, except being separated.
Today everyone goes to the country to enjoy nature
No heart is left in town for you to venture.
I had promised to tell all my sorrows when you come
What can I say since sorrows leave me as you come.
The candle should be taken and extinguished outside
So the neighbours do not learn that you are inside.
Sa'di is not one who would break out of your chain
He knows he is better your captive than free in pain.
People tell me to give my heart to someone else
But I will not seek yet another love elsewhere.[60]

آبگینه شکسته
تو هیچ عهد نبستی که عاقبت نشکستی
مرا بر آتش سوزان نشاندی و ننشستی
بنای مهر نمودی که پایدار نماند
مرا به بند بستی خود از کمند بجستی
دلم شکستی و رفتی خلاف شرط مودت
به احتیاط گذر کن که آبگینه شکستی
چراغ چون تو نباشد به هیچ خانه ولیکن
کس این سرای نبندد در این چنین که تو بستی
گرم عذاب نمایی به داغ و درد جدایی
شکنجه صبر ندارم، بریز خونم و رستی
بیا که ما سر هستی و کبریا و رعونت
به زیر پای نهادیم و پای بر سر هستی
گرت به گوشه چشمی نظر بود به اسیران
دوای درد من اول، که بی گناه بخستی
هر آن کست که ببیند روا بود که بگوید
که من بهشت بدیدم به راستی و درستی
گرت کسی بپرستد ملامتش نکنم من
تو هم در آینه بنگر که خویشتن بپرستی
عجب مدار که سعدی به یاد دوست بنالد
که عشق موجب شوق است و خمر علت مستی

Shattered mirror

No pledge you ever made you did not break
You led me into burning fire and left
You laid the foundation of a transient love
Putting me in chains and breaking out of the trap.
You broke my heart unkindly and left
Walk carefully, then, as a mirror you've shattered
No light like you is found in any home
Yet no-one stays indoors as regularly as you.
If you wish to cause me the pain of separation
I can't bear torture; kill me and enjoy your liberation
See that I have suppressed pride and arrogance
And have even repudiated my whole existence.
If you have the slightest care for prisoners
Treat this innocent whom you hurt first
Anyone seeing you would be right in saying
That he's seen Heaven well and truly.
I do not blame anyone worshipping you
If you look at the mirror even you will do
No wonder Sa'di mourns in your absence
For love brings passion and wine drunkenness.[61]

آن صبح کجا رفت

دوش بی روی تو آتش به سرم بر می شد
و آبی از دیده می آمد که زمین تر می شد
تا به افسوس به پایان نرود عمر عزیز
همه شب ذکر تو می رفت و مکرر می شد
چون شب آمد همه را دیده بیارامد و من
گفتی اندر بن مویم سر نشتر می شد
آن نه می بود که دور از نظرت می خوردم
خون دل بود که از دیده به ساغر می شد
از خیال تو به هر سو که نظر می کردم
پیش چشمم در و دیوار مصور می شد
چشم مجنون چو بخفتی همه لیلی دیدی
مدعی بود اگرش خواب میسر می شد
هوش می آمد و می رفت و نه دیدار ترا
می بدیدم نه خیالم ز برابر می شد
گاه چون عود بر آتش دل تنگم می سوخت
گاه چون مجمره ام دود به سر بر می شد
یا رب آن صبح کجا رفت که شب های دگر
نفسی می زد و آفاق منور می شد
سعدیا عقد ثریا مگر امشب بگسیخت
ورنه هر شب به گریبان افق بر می شد

Where is that dawn?

Thinking of you at night my head was on fire
And tears from my eyes flooded the earth
All night I was speaking your name
So that dear life would not have gone to waste.
At night everyone's eyes chance to rest
Not me, almost as if needles were piercing my head
What I was drinking without you was not wine
It was my heart's blood pouring into the cup.
Thinking of you, everywhere I looked
I saw nothing but wall after wall after wall
With his eyes shut, Majnun could see none but Leyli
He wasn't a true lover if he'd slept peacefully.
I could not see you, asleep or awake
Yet your image remained in my head
Now my heart burns as the incense burns
Now smoke went up my head as if it were fire.
God, where did that dawn go when the other nights
It breathed a while and the horizons were alight?
Sa'di the Pleiades seems to have lost its necklace tonight
Since it used to hang from the horizon every night.[62]

روز و شب مستم
به خاک پای عزیزت که عهد نشکستم
ز من بریدی و با هیچ کس نپیوستم
کجا روم که بمیرم بر آستان امید
اگر به دامن وصلت نمی رسد دستم
شگفت مانده ام از بامداد روز وداع
که برنخاست قیامت چو بی تو بنشستم
بلای عشق تو نگذاشت پارسا در پارس
یکی منم که ندانم نماز چون بستم
نماز مست شریعت روا نمی دارد
نماز من که پذیرد که روز و شب مستم
چنین که دست خیالت گرفت دامن من
چه بودی ار برسیدی به دامنت دستم
من از کجا و تمنای وصل تو ز کجا
اگر چه آب حیاتی هلاک خود جستم
اگر خلاف تو بودست در دلم همه عمر
نه نیک رفت خطا کردم و ندانستم
بکش چنانکه تو دانی که سعدی آن کس نیست
که با وجود تو دعوی کند که من هستم

Always drunk

By the dust under your feet I did not break my pledge
You broke with me and I didn't turn to anyone else.
Where can I go and die at the threshold of hope
Now that I cannot be with you, at your feet?
I wonder why on the day of our separation
No storm broke out when you left me alone.
The sin of your love spared no-one pious in Pars
Except me, and I don't know how I said my prayers.
Religious law forbids praying while inebriate
Mine will not be heard as I am always drunk.
What would be wrong if I took your hand
Just like your love has gripped me in its hand?
Having you in my arms, what ambition!
You're the elixir of life yet I seek my destruction.
Even if I was inconstant once in my life
It was not intentional, but unconsciously done.
Come and kill me as you know how, since
As long as you are, Sa'di cannot claim to exist.[63]

زندان عشق
شب فراق که داند که تا سحر چند است
مگر کسی که به زندان عشق در بند است
گرفتم از غم دل راه بوستان گیرم
کدام سرو به بالای دوست ماند است؟
پیام من که رساند به یار مهرگسل
که بر شکستی و ما را هنوز پیوند است
قسم به جان تو گفتن طریق عزت نیست
به خاک پای تو و آن هم عظیم سوگند است
که با شکستن پیمان و برگرفتن دل
هنوز دیده به دیدارت آرزومند است
بیا که بر سر کویت بساط چهره ماست
به جای خاک که در زیر پایت افکندست
خیال روی تو بیخ امید بنشاندست
بلای عشق تو بنیاد صبر برکندست
عجب در آن که تو مجموع و گر قیاس کنی
به زیر هر خم مویت دلی پراکندست
اگر برهنه نباشی که شخص بنمایی
گمان برند که پیراهنت گل آکندست
ز دست رفته نه تنها منم در این سودا
چه دست ها که ز دست تو بر خداوند است
ز ضعف طاقت آهم نماند و ترسم خلق
گمان برند که سعدی ز دوست خرسند است

Prisoner of love

He would know how long is the night of separation
Who is fettered in love's prison.
Suppose I go to the garden to overcome sadness
What flower can compensate me for your absence?
Someone take the message to my inconstant lover
That despite her leaving me I still belong to her.
To swear by you is an insult, so I swear
By the dust of your feet – itself a great oath –
That despite your inconstancy and heart-breaking
My eyes are still longing to be set on thee.
Step out of your home and see my face
Is spread for you to step on instead of dust
The hope of seeing you has taken deep roots
But the calamity of your love has uprooted all patience.
Strange that you are so serene and composed
While for every hair on you so many hearts are shattered
If you don't go naked to show your body
They'd think that your gown is flowery.
I am not the only one lost in thought of you
There are many hands raised to God because of you
Weakness does not let me sigh, and I'm afraid
That people might think Sa'di is not unhappy without you.[64]

بند تنهایی
فراق دوستانش باد و یاران
که ما را دور کرد از دوستداران
دلم در بند تنهایی بفرسود
چو بلبل در قفس روز بهاران
هلاک ما چنان مهمل گرفتند
که قتل مور در پای سواران
به خیل هر که می آیم به زنهار
نمی بینم بجز زنهار خواران
ندانستم که در پایان صحبت
چنین باشد وفای حق گذاران
به گنج شایگان افتاده بودم
ندانستم که بر گنجند ماران
دلا گر دوستی داری به ناچار
بباید بردنت جور هزاران
خلاف شرط یاران است سعدی
که برگردند روز تیرباران
چه خوش باشد سری در پای یاری
به اخلاص و ارادت جان سپاران

Forlorn captivity

I am kept afar from my sweetheart
May he who is behind it suffer the same fate
In my loneliness my heart burns with rage
Like a spring nightingale kept in a cage.
They thought as little of our life
As that of an ant trampled under a hoof
Wherever I turn to for help and protection
I receive nothing but an untrustworthy reception.
I did not know that by friendship's end
This is the appreciation that is offered
I thought I had found an immense treasure
Not knowing that it is guarded by snakes.
Although when you love you must expect
To suffer a thousand oppressions and cruelties
Yet it is not the way of lovers, Sa'di,
To turn their back at times of adversity.
Better to put one's head under the beloved's foot
And thus die with faith and sincerity.[65]

منزلگه احرار
خرم آن بقعه که آرامگه یار آنجاست
راحت جان و شفای دل بیمار آنجاست
من در این جای همین صورت بی جانم و بس
دلم آنجاست که آن دلبر عیار آنجاست
تنم اینجاست سقیم و دلم آنجاست مقیم
فلک اینجاست ولی کوکب سیار آنجاست
آخر ای باد صبا بویی اگر می آری
سوی شیراز گذر کن که مرا یار آنجاست
درد دل پیش که گویم غم دل با که خورم
روم آنجا که مرا محرم اسرار آنجاست
نکند میل دل من به تماشای چمن
که تماشای دل آنجاست که دلبر آنجاست
سعدی این منزل ویران چه کنی جای تو نیست
رخت بربند که منزلگه احرار آنجاست

Abode of the free

Green is the valley where the beloved resides
And where there is cure for heavy hearts
Here I am just this soulless figure
My heart is where that enticing sweetheart figures.
My sick body is here and my heart is there:
The sky is here but that wondering star is there
O morning breeze if you bring a fragrance
Blow through Shiraz since my sweetheart is there.
There is no-one to whom I can open my heart
I must go where the keeper of my secrets lies
I have no desire to see gardens green
I long to be where my sweetheart is.
Why remain in this worthless ruin, Sa'di,
Get up and go to the abode of the free.[66]

حد جنایت

بیا که نوبت صلح است و دوستی و عنایت
به شرط آنکه نگوییم از آنچه رفت حکایت
برین یکی شده بودم که گرد عشق نگردم
قضاء عشق درآمد بدوخت چشم درایت
ملامت من مسکین کسی کند که نداند
که عشق تا به چه حد است و حسن تا به چه غایت
ز حرص من ز چه گشاید (؟) تو ره به خویشتنم ده
که چشم سعی ضعیف است بی چراغ هدایت
مرا به دست تو خوش تر هلاک جان گرامی
هزار باره، که رفتن به دیگری به حمایت
جنایتی که بکردم اگر درست بباشد
فراق روی تو چندین بس است حد جنایت
به هیچ روی نشاید خلاف رای تو گفتن
کجا برم گله از دست پادشاه ولایت
به هیچ صورتی اندر نباشد این همه معنی
به هیچ سورتی اندر نباشد این همه آیت
کمال حسن وجودت به وصف راست نیاید
مگر هم آینه گوید چنان که هست حکایت
مرا سخن به نهایت رسید و فکر به پایان
هنوز وصف جمالت نمی رسد به نهایت
فراق نامه سعدی به هیچ گوش نیامد
که دردی از سخنانش در او نکرد سرایت

Vengeance constrained

Come, it's time for peace, friendship and kindness
But not to talk about what went in the past
I was determined not to fall in love
Fate brought love and shut my eyes.
He would admonish me who does not know
How much I love and how beautiful are you
My eagerness is helpless without your sight
For a weak eye will need help from light.
I would much rather be killed by your hands
Than seek support from anyone else
Even if I have committed a crime
Not seeing you is retribution enough.
I cannot possibly contradict your will:
To whom can one complain of the king?
No-one's appearance hides as much reality as yours
Neither does a holy chapter contain so many verses.
Your perfect beauty is beyond description
Perhaps only the mirror can create a true reflection
My thoughts and words reached their end
Yet appreciation of your beauty never ends.
No-one listens to the story of Sa'di's separation
Since his pains do not bring from her any recognition.[67]

وجود حاضر غیب
از هر چه می رود سخن دوست خوشترست
پیغام آشنا نفس روح پرورست
هرگز وجود حاضر غیب شنیده ای؟
من در میان جمع و دلم جای دیگرست
شاهد که در میان نبود شمع گو بمیر
ور هست اگر چراغ نباشد منورست
ابنای روزگار به صحرا روند و باغ
صحرا و باغ زنده دلان کوی دلبرست
جان قدم میروم که در اندازمش ز شوق
درمانده ام هنوز که نزلی محقرست
کاش آن به خشم رفته ما آشتی کنان
باز آمدی که دیده مشتاق بر درست
جانا دلم چو عود بر آتش بسوختی
وین دم که می زنم ز غمت دود مجمرست
شبهای بی توام شب گور است در خیال
ور بی تو بامداد کنم روز محشرست
گیسوت عنبرینه گردن تمام بود
معشوق خوبروی چه حاجت به زیورست
سعدی خیال بیهده بستی امید وصل
هجرت بکشت و وصل هنوزت مصورست؟
زنهار از این امید درازت که در دلست
هیهات از این خیال محالت که در سرست

Absent presence

Naught is more joyous than the beloved's word
A message from her is a breath that lifts up the soul.
Can you believe one to be both present and absent?
I am with others but my heart is somewhere else.
When the beloved is absent let the candle die
And when she is present she shines like a light.
People go out to the garden and countryside
The garden of lovers is where the loved one resides.
Ecstatically I wish to sacrifice my life for her
My only regret is that it is an unworthy gift to her.
She left in anger, would that she come back to make up
And see my hopeful eyes permanently fixed on her path.
Beloved, you put me like aloes wood on fire
It's smoke I breath, lamenting our separation dire.
Without you I feel buried every night
Just as rising is resurrection-like.
The chain of your hair is a perfect necklace
For a beautiful angel is in need of no jewels.
There was no hope, Sa'di, in your longing for union
You died of separation and still dream of union?
Alas, you must now pity your hopeful heart
And mourn the impossible wish that you have.[68]

یاران صبوحی ام کجایند
گر غصه روزگار گویم
بس قصه بی شمار گویم
یک عمر هزار سال باید
تا من یکی از هزار گویم
چشمم به زبان حال گوید
نی آنکه به اختیار گویم
بر من دل انجمن بسوزد
گر درد فراق یار گویم
مرغان چمن فغان برآرند
گر فرقت نوبهار گویم
یاران صبوحی ام کجایند
تا درد دل خمار گویم
کس نیست که دل سوی من آرد
تا غصه روزگار گویم
درد دل بی قرار سعدی
هم با دل بی قرار گویم.

Where are my drinking companions?

If I describe the pains of separation
I'll have to tell the story of damnation.
It will take me a thousand years
To tell about one of a thousand tears.
My sadness is evident from my eyes
No need to say it by mouth.
Friends would have pity on me
If I described the pain of being lonely.
Even the garden birds will cry
If I tell them about the loss of my spring.
Where are my fellow morning-drinkers
So I can tell them about the morning after.
No-one's heart is open to mine
So that I can tell him the sorrows of life.
No choice but to describe the pain in my head
Only to my own pain-struck heart.[69]

کمند شوق
گر از جفای تو روزی دلم بیازارد
کمند شوق کشانم به صلح بازآرد
ز درد عشق تو دوشم امید صبح نبود
اسیر عشق چه تاب شب دراز آرد
دلی عجب نبود گر بسوخت کاتش عشق
چه جای موم که پولاد در گداز آرد
تویی که گر بخرامد درخت قامت تو
ز رشک سرو روان را به اهتزاز آرد
دگر به روی خود از خلق در بخواهم بست
مگر کسی ز توام مژده ای فرازآرد
اگر قبول کنی سرنهیم بر قدمت
چو بت پرست که در پیش بت نماز آرد
یکی به سمع رضا گوش دل به سعدی دار
که سوز عشق سخن های دلنواز آرد

The pull of desire

If by your unkindness my heart is hurt
The pull of desire will make it submit
I could not hope to see the day last night
Being a captive of love with pain in my heart.
No wonder that my heart burns since
The fire of love melts steel let alone wax
You are the one who if you move your body
You will shake up the cypress tree with envy.
I am decided to give up seeing people
Unless someone brings me good news of you
If you wish I will put my head at your feet
And worship you as they worship idols.
For once at least listen to what Sa'di says
Because the fire of love makes pleasing words.[70]

سیمرغ و زاغ
ای کاش زندگانی من در دهان توست
تیر هلاک ظاهر من در کمان توست
گر برقعی فرونگذاری بدین جمال
در شهر هر که کشته شود در ضمان توست
تشبیه روی تو نکنم من به آفتاب
کاین مدح آفتاب، نه تعظیم شأن توست
گر یک نظر به گوشه چشم ارادتی
با ما کنی و گر نکنی حکم ازآن توست
هر روز خلق را سر یاری و صاحبیست
ما را همین سر است که بر آستان توست
بسیار دیده ایم درختان میوه دار
زین به ندیده ایم که در بوستان توست
گر دست دوستان نرسد باغ را چه جرم؟
منعی که می رود گنه از باغبان توست
بسیار در دل آمد اندیشه ها و رفت
نقشی که آن نمی رود از دل نشان توست
با من هزارنوبت اگر دشمنی کنی
ای دوست همچنان دل من مهربان توست
سعدی به قدر خویش تمنای وصل کن
سیمرغ ما چه لایق زاغ آشیان توست

Simorgh and the magpie

The elixir of my life is in your mouth
And in your bow is the arrow of my death
Cover that beauty of yours with a veil
Or the death of your lovers will be your fault.
I will not compare your face to the sun
Since it will honour not you but the sun
Whether you give or don't give me a look of approval
The command is yours, do it or not.
People daily look for friends and lords
I only have this head which is at your threshold
Trees full of fruits I have seen many
But those in your orchard are better than any.
No offence if I cannot make it to the garden
You being the gardener, the barrier is you
Many thoughts came and went in my mind
The one that would not go is the picture of you.
Even if you offend me a thousand times,
Friend, my heart is still filled with love for you
Sa'di, you must seek love as much as you are worth
How can a magpie seek the love of Simorgh?[71]

وداع

بگذار تا بگریم چون ابر در بهاران
کز سنگ ناله خیزد روز وداع یاران
هر کو شراب فرقت روزی چشیده باشد
داند که سخت باشد قطع امیدواران
با ساربان بگویید احوال آب چشمم
تا بر شتر نبندد محمل به روز باران
بگذاشتند ما را در دیده آب حسرت
گریان چو در قیامت چشم گناهکاران
ای صبح شب نشینان جانم بطاقت آمد
از بس که دیر ماندی چون شام روزه داران
چندین که بر شمردم از ماجرای عشقت
اندوه دل نگفتم الا یک از هزاران
سعدی به روزگاران مهری نشسته بر دل
بیرون نمی توان کرد الا به روزگاران
چندت کنم حکایت شرح این قدر کفایت
باقی نمی توان گفت الا به غمگساران

Ceremonies of farewell

Let me cry hard like the spring cloud
Farewell to friends makes stones mourn aloud
Anyone having once tasted the wine of separation
Knows the pains of losing hope and aspiration.
Tell the camel-driver about the water in my eye
To put the water-skin aside when it pours from the sky
They left us, eyes filled with the water of desire,
Weeping like the sinful at Resurrection with hellfire.
O morning of the night-dwellers please begin
You're as late as the night of those who fast
So much that I have said about your love's story
Is but one in a thousand of my grief and misery.
Years have embedded such affection in your heart,
Sa'di, that only years could remove from your heart.
I have told you enough, now I will be coy
What's left I'll tell friends whose sympathy I enjoy.[72]

چو بلبل آمدمت
من از تو صبر ندارم که بی تو بنشینم
کسی دگر نتوانم که بر تو بگزینم
بپرس حال من آخر چو بگذری روزی
که چون همی گذرد روزگار مسکینم
من اهل دوزخم ار بی تو زنده خواهم شد
که در بهشت نیارد خدای غمگینم
ندانمت که چه گویم تو هر دو چشم منی
که بی وجود شریفت جهان نمی بینم
چو روی دوست نبینی جهان ندیدن به
شب فرق منه شمع پیش بالینم
ضرورت است که عهد وفا بسر برمت
وگر جفا بسرآید هزار چندینم
نه هاونم که بنالم بکوفتی ای یار
چو دیگ بر سر آتش نشان که بنشینم
بگرد بر سرم ای آسیای دور زمان
به هر جفا که توانی، که سنگ زیرینم
چو بلبل آمدمت تا چو گل ثنا گویم
چو لاله لال بکردی زبان تحسینم
مرا پلنگ به سرپنجه، ای نگار نکشت
تو می کشی به سرپنجه نگارینم
چو ناف آهو خونم بسوخت در دل تنگ
برفت در همه آفاق بوی مشکینم
هنر بیار و زبان آوری مکن سعدی
چه حاجت است بگوید شکر که شیرینم

I came to you like a nightingale

I have no patience to be without you
Nor can I put anyone above you.
Do ask how I am as you pass one day
And see how miserable are my days.
Without you God will put me in hell
At the Resurrection, not miserable in heaven.
What can I say, you are both my eyes
Since without you I cannot see the sun rise.
Not seeing the friend's face, better not to see at all
At the night of separation don't put candles on the wall.
I pledge to remain constant in every way
But if you come it'll doubly make my day.
I will not mourn if you beat me like a mortar
Put me like a pan on the fire and I'll settle down.
Turn like the watermill's upper granite
As hard as you can as I am under it.
I tried to sing like a nightingale to your flower
Like a dumb tulip you stopped me admiring you.
Beloved, I was not killed by the leopard's claws
And yet you are killing me with your lovely paws.
Blood burnt in my heart like the navel of a deer
The aroma of musk spread everywhere.
Stop playing with words, Sa'di, show art
Sugar is indeed sweet but that apart.[73]

مجال صبر تنگ آمد

چنان در قید مهرت پای بندم
که گوئی آهوی سر در کمندم
گهی بر درد بی درمان بگریم
گهی بر حال بی سامان بخندم
مرا هوشی نماند از عشق و گوشی
که پند هوشمندان کاربندم
مجال صبر تنگ آمد به یکبار
حدیث عشق بر صحرا فکندم
نه مجنونم که دل بردارم از دوست
مده گر عاقلی ای خواجه پندم
چنین صورت نبندد هیچ نقاش
معاذ الله من این صورت ببندم
چه جانها در غمت فرسود و تن ها
نه تنها من اسیر و مستمندم
تو هم بازآمدی ناچار و ناکام
اگر بازآمدی بخت بلندم
گر آوازم دهی من خفته در گور
برآساید روان دردمندم
سری دارم فدای خاک پایت
گر آسایش رسانی ور گزندم
وگر در رنج سعدی راحت توست
من این بیداد بر خود می پسندم

I miss you so much

I am so trapped in your love
As if a deer lassoed by want
Now I weep from my endless pain
Now I laugh at my ruined state.
I have no sense in me left
To listen to the advice of the deft
I missed you so much in the end
That, like Majnun, I took to the desert.
I am not mad enough to give up her love
Stop advising me if you are wise
No artist could paint a face as fine
I'd never give up that face divine.
What bodies and souls were lost for you
So I am not the only one, others too
You will come back only when
My good luck returns to me.
Even lying in my grave if you call
It'll soothe my painful soul
Whether you bring me pain or comfort
My head is not worth the dust under your feet.
And if your comfort is in Sa'di's pain
Of this injustice I will not disdain.[74]

ETHICAL/MYSTICAL

مکان آدمیت
تن آدمی شریف است به جان آدمیت
نه همین لباس زیباست نشان آدمیت
اگر آدمی به چشم است و دهان و گوش و بینی
چه میان نقش دیوار و میان آدمیت
خور و خواب و خشم و شهوت شغب است و جهل و ظلمت
حیوان خبر ندارد ز جهان آدمیت
به حقیقت آدمی باش وگرنه مرغ باشد
که همان سخن بگوید به زبان آدمیت
مگر آدمی نبودی که اسیر دیو گشتی
که فرشته ره ندارد به مکان آدمیت
اگر این درنده خویی ز طبیعتت بمیرد
همه عمر زنده باشی به روان آدمیت
رسد آدمی به جایی که بجز خدا نبیند
بنگر که تا چه حد است مکان آدمیت
طیران مرغ دیدی، تو ز پای بند شهوت
بدرآی تا ببینی طیران آدمیت
نه بیان فضل کردم که نصیحت تو گفتم
هم از آدمی شنیدیم بیان آدمیت

The place of humanity

The human body is ennobled by the human soul
You will not be human just wearing a nice shawl
If eye, mouth, ear and nose define a human being
What is the difference between man and a picture
    on the wall?
Eating, sleeping, anger, passion are darkness and ignorance
Animals know not of the world of humanity at all
Try to be a human being in reality, otherwise a parrot
May mimic human beings' language, speech and call.
How as a human became you captive to demons?
Not even angels can rise up to man's potential
If the cannibalism in your nature dies and disappears
You will be always alive through the human soul.
Man may reach a point of seeing no-one but God
See how man's place may be mighty and high
Birds fly, free yourself from fetters of passion
To see how human beings can fly like them all.
I did not claim to be virtuous, just gave you advice
It was from humanity itself that we learned about man.[75]

ملک گدایان
چون عیش گدایان به جهان سلطنتی نیست
مجموع تر از ملک رضا مملکتی نیست
گر منزلتی هست کسی را مگر آن است
کاندر نظر هیچ کسش منزلتی نیست
هر کس صفتی دارد و رنگی و نشانی
تو ترک صفت کن که از این به صفتی نیست
پوشیده کسی بینی فردای قیامت
کامروز برهنست و بر او عاریتی نیست
آن کس که در او معرفتی هست کدام است؟
آنست که با هیچ کسش معرفتی نیست
سنگی و گیاهی که در آن خاصیتی هست
از آدمی به که در او منفعتی نیست
درویش تو در مصلحت خویش ندانی
خوش باش اگرت نیست، که بی مصلحتی نیست
آن دوست نباشد که شکایت کند از دوست
بر خون که دلارام بریزد دیتی نیست
راه ادب این است که سعدی به تو آموخت
گر گوش بداری به از این تربیتی نیست

The kingdom of beggars

There is no life as royal as that of beggars
No kingdom is more secure than contentment
If anyone has real dignity it is he
Whom others treat with indignity.
Everyone has a character, a colour, a creed
Give them all up, that is the best thing
On the Day of Judgement he will be clothed
Who in this world is naked, is not adorned.
Who has real knowledge of the world?
It is he who knows no-one and is all on his own
The stone and the vegetation which are of some use
Are better than the man who is not useful to others.
You don't know, O dervish, what is expedient
Rejoice that your poverty is not inexpedient
He who complains of the beloved is no lover
There is no compensation for being killed by the lover.
Good manners are these which are taught by Sa'di
If you seek education there is none better.[76]

کشته شمشیر عشق
آن را که جای نیست همه شهر جای اوست
درویش هر کجا که شب آید سرای اوست
بی خانمان که هیچ ندارد بجز خدای
او را گدا مگوی که سلطان گدای اوست
مرد خدا به مشرق و مغرب غریب نیست
هر جا که می رود همه ملک خدای اوست
آن کز توانگری و بزرگی و خواجگی
بیگانه شد، به هر که رسد آشنای اوست
کوتاه دیدگان همه راحت طلب کنند
عارف بلا، که راحت او در بلای اوست
عاشق که بر مشاهده دوست دست یافت
در هر چه بعد از آن نگرد اژدهای اوست
بگذار هر چه داری و بگذر که هیچ نیست
این پنج روزه عمر که مرگ از قفای اوست
هر آدمی که کشته شمشیر عشق شد
گو غم مخور که ملک ابد خونبهای اوست
از دست دوست هر چه ستانی شکر بود
سعدی رضای خود مطلب چون رضای اوست

Martyr to love

The whole town belongs to the homeless person
The dervish is at home anywhere that night falls.
Do not call the homeless person who has no-one but God
A beggar, for the sultan is below him in the sight of God.
The man of God is no stranger in east and west
It is the kingdom of God wherever he can rest.
He who is stripped of riches, lordship and power
Is known and familiar to everyone he encounters.
The narrow-minded merely seek joy and comfort
The *aref* seeks discomfort, which is his comfort.
The lover who managed to observe Him
If he sought anything else it would be his ruin.
Leave all you have and leave, for this short life
Is nothing, and is followed by nothing but demise.
Whoever became a martyr to the Kingdom of Love
Need not worry for he will inherit the Kingdom Eternal.
Whatever the Beloved gives is like sugar sweet
Sa'di, seek not your contentment except by His Will.[77]

بگذار تا بیفتد و بیند سزای خویش
ای روبهک چرا ننشینی به جای خویش
با شیر پنجه کردی و دیدی سزای خویش
دشمن به دشمن آن نپسندد که بی خرد
با نفس خود کند به هوای مراد خویش
از دست دیگران چه شکایت کند کسی
سیلی به دست خویش زند بر قفای خویش
دزد از جفای شحنه چه فریاد می کند
گو گردنت نمی زند الا جفای خویش
خونت برای قالی سلطان بریختند
ابله چرا نخفتی بر بوریای خویش
گر هر دو دیده هیچ نبیند به اتفاق
بهتر ز دیده ای که نبیند خطای خویش
چاه است و راه و دیده بینا و آفتاب
تا آدمی نگاه کند پیش پای خویش
چندین چراغ دارد و بی راهه می رود
بگذار تا بیفتد و بیند سزای خویش
با دیگران بگوی که ظالم به چه فتاد
تا چاه دیگران نکنند از برای خویش
گر گوش دل به گفته سعدی کند کسی
اول رضای حق طلبد پس رضای خویش

Let him fall...

Little fox, why did you not know your place
You fought with a lion and got what you deserved
Not even your enemy would wish for what
You bring onto yourself by your whims.
He who brings disaster onto himself
Cannot complain of the ill intentions of others
Why would a thief mind the punishment of the law
When it is he who brings it on himself?
They let your blood for the Sultan's carpet
Why, idiot, did you not sleep on your straw mat?
If a person completely lost his sight
It would be better than him not seeing his fault.
There are holes on the road but also light
So one can clearly see holes from a height
Light everywhere and yet he takes the wrong path
Let him fall, then, and reap the punishment he must.
Tell people that the unjust dug their own graves
So they don't go around and dig graves for others
Anyone whose heart listens to Sa'di's advice
Will not put his own will above God's.[78]

بنیاد بقا محکم از اوست
به جهان خرم از آنم که جهان خرم از اوست
عاشقم بر همه عالم که همه عالم از اوست
به غنیمت شمر ای دوست دم عیسی صبح
تا دل مرده مگر زنده کنی کاین دم از اوست
نه فلک راست مسلم نه ملک را حاصل
آنچه در سر سویدای بنی آدم از اوست
به حلاوت بخورم زهر که شاهد ساقیست
به ارادت ببرم درد که درمانم از اوست
زخم خونینم اگر به نشود به باشد
خنک آن زخم که هر لحظه مرا مرهم از اوست
غم و شادی بر عارف چه تفاوت دارد
ساقیا باده بده شادی آن کاین غم از اوست
پادشاهی و گدایی بر ما یکسان است
که بر این در همه را پشت عبادت خم از اوست
سعدیا گر بکند سیل فنا خانه عمر
دل قوی دار که بنیاد بقا محکم از اوست

The foundation of being
I am cheerful in this lush world of His
I love it because it all comes from Him.
Value, my friend, the Jesus-like morning breath
Which will bring life to your dead heart.
Neither the universe nor angels know at all
What deep secrets He holds for us all.
Poison is sweet, thinking He is the Saqi
I'll happily bear the pain since He is also the cure.
I am happy that my bloody wound does not heal
So I constantly receive healing from Him.
To the *aref* sadness and joy are the same
Let's drink happily that the sadness is from Him.
Being a beggar or a king is all the same to me
Since everyone's back is bent before Him.
Sa'di, even if the flood of death uproots the abode
Be sure that the foundation of being is firm from Him.[79]

با تو همین ماجرا رود

بسیار سال ها به سر خاک ما رود
کاین آب چشمه آید و باد صبا رود
این پنج روزه روزه مهلت ایام، آدمی
بر خاک دیگران به تکبر چرا رود
ای دوست بر جنازه دشمن چو بگذری
شادی مکن که با تو همین ماجرا رود
دامن کشان که می رود امروز بر زمین
فردا غبار کالبدش در هوا رود
خاکت در استخوان رود ای نفس شوخ چشم
مانند سرمه-دان که در آن توتیا رود
دنیا حریف سفله و معشوق بی وفاست
چون می رود هر آینه بگذار تا رود
این است حال تن که تو بینی به زیر خاک
تا جان نازنین که برآید کجا رود
بر سایبان حسن عمل اعتماد نیست
سعدی مگر به سایه لطف خدا رود
یا رب مگیر بنده مسکین و دست گیر
کز تو کرم برآید و از ما خطا رود

The same fate shall befall you

Years will pass on the dust of our dead rows
While the spring still fills and the breeze still blows.
In these few days of life why should one treat
Other people with arrogance and conceit?
Friend, when you pass by your enemy's funeral cortège
Do not jump for joy for you'll be just the same one day.
Now you walk on dust with such pride
In the air tomorrow will be the mist of your own dust.
Your bones will fill with dust, O pleasure-seeking soul
Just as the make-up box fills with blue vitriol.
Life is a base partner and an inconstant lover
As it moves on just let it go forward.
You can imagine the state of the body in the grave
One wonders where the dear soul will have gone.
One cannot even trust the reward of good deeds,
Sa'di, unless it is combined with God's grace.
O God, forgive your wretched servants and help
Since from us are the errors, from you the grace.[80]

عالم درویشان
ای که انکار کنی عالم درویشان را
تو ندانی که چه سودا و سرست ایشان را
گنج آزادگی و کنج قناعت ملکیست
که به شمشیر میسر نشود سلطان را
طلب منصب فانی نکند صاحب عقل
عاقل آن است که اندیشه کند پایان را
جمع کردند و نهادند و به حسرت رفتند
وین چه دارد که به حسرت بگذارد آن را
آن بدر می رود از باغ به دلتنگی و داغ
وین به بازوی فرح می شکند زندان را
دستگاهی نه که تشویش قیامت باشد
مرغ آبیست چه اندیشه کند طوفان را
جان بیگانه ستاند ملک الموت به زجر
زجر حاجت نبود عاشق جان افشان را
چشم همت نه به دنیا که به عقبی نبود
عارف عاشق شوریده سرگردان را
در ازل بود که پیمان محبت بستند
نشکند مرد اگرش سر برود پیمان را
عاشقی سوخته ای بی سر و سامان دیدم
گفتم ای یار مکن بر سر فکرت جان را
نفسی سرد برآورد ضعیف از سر درد
گفت بگذار من بی سر و بی سامان را
پند دلبند تو در گوش من آید هیهات
من که بر درد حریصم چه کنم درمان را
سعدیا عمر عزیز است به غفلت مگذار
وقت فرصت نشود فوت مگر نادان را

The world of dervishes

You who deny the world of dervishes
Do not know of their beliefs and wishes,
The treasure of needlessness and contentment is in a place
Which the sultan and his kingdom cannot reach by force.
No-one with reason would look for transient power
One who has reason would contemplate the dire end
The rich man accumulated and ruefully disappeared
But the dervish has nothing to leave behind with remorse.
The former leaves the garden of life full of regret
Whereas the latter breaks free from material living
He has no reason to worry about the Day of Judgement
Like a seagull which is not afraid of storm.
The Angel of Death kills strangers painfully
No pain though for the dervish familiar to Him
A dervish lover is so free from need and greed
That he wants neither this world nor even the other.
The pact of love was made at the dawn of creation
He would not break his word even on pain of death
I saw a lover, burnt by experience with nowhere to go
I told him, Friend do not sacrifice your life for your beliefs.
Ah, he said, weakly with a cold painful sigh,
Please leave me alone, I who have nothing of my own,
I will never listen to your good word of advice
For I seek pain and need no cure otherwise.
Life is dear, Sa'di, to be lived wise
Time is not wasted except by the unwise.[81]

Notes

PREFACE

1. I have tried to rectify this gross neglect in a series of 20 articles in Persian, published in the literary journal *Iranshenasi*, which were later put together in a single volume, *Sa'di Sha'er-e Eshq o Zendegi*; in my book in English, *Sa'di, The Poet of Life, Love and Compassion*; and in an anthology of his works, *Golchin-e Sa'di*.

INTRODUCTION

1. See Mohammad Qazvini, 'Mamduhin-e Sa'di', in Habib Yaghma'i (ed.), *Sa'di-Nameh*, Tehran: Ministry of Education, 1938.
2. See *The Travels of Ibn Battuta*, ed. Tim Macintosh-Smith, London: Picador, 2002.
3. See Homa Katouzian, *Sa'di: The Poet of Life, Love and Compassion*, Oxford: Oneworld, 2006.
4. See Homa Katouzian, 'Classical Persian Literature: Form and Substance', in *Iran: Politics, History and Literature*, London and New York: Routledge, 2013.
5. Edward G. Browne, *A Literary History of Persia*, Volume II: *From Firdawsi to Sa'di*, Cambridge: Cambridge University Press, 1923.
6. See Katouzian, *Sa'di: The Poet of Life, Love and Compassion*, ch. 1; Homa Katouzian, *Sa'di, Sha'er-e Eshq o Zendegi*, Tehran: Nashr-e Markaz, 2006, ch. 7.
7. See Rashid Yasemi in Yaghma'i (ed.), *Sa'di Nameh*.
8. Mohammad Ali Foroughi (ed.), *Ghazaliyat-e Sa'di*, Tehran: Berukhim, 1939; and *Kolliyat-e Sa'di*, ed. Baha al-Din Khorramshahi, Tehran: Amir Kabir, 1977.
9. Habib Yaghma'i (ed.), *Ghazaliyat-e Sa'di*, Tehran: Moasseseh-ye Tahqiqat va Motale'at-e Farhangi, 1982.
10. Ali Dashti, *Qalamrov-e Sa'di*, Tehran: Keyhan, 1959, pp. 364–96.
11. Ibid., p. 365.
12. Ibid., pp. 365–6.
13. Gholamhoseyn Yusefi (ed.), *Ghazalha-ye Sa'di*, Tehran: Elmi, 2006.
14. Sa'id Hamidiyan, *Sa'di dar Ghazal*, Tehran: Nashr-e Qatreh, 2002.
15. See Katouzian, *Sa'di: The Poet of Life*, ch. 3.
16. See Katouzian, *Sa'di, Sha'er-e Eshq o Zendegi*, chs 14–19.
17. Homa Katouzian, *Golchin-e Sa'di: Gozideh-ye Golestan, Ghazal-ha, Bustan, Qasideh-ha*, Tehran: Nashr-e Markaz, 2009.
18. Henri Massé, *Essai sur le Poète Saadi*, Paris: Paul Geuthner, 1919; Persian translation by Mohammad Hasan Mahdavi Ardebili and Gholamhoseyn Yusefi, *Tahqiq darbareh-ye Sa'di*, Tehran: Tus, 1990.
19. Quoted by Scott Horton in 'Emerson's Saadi', http://harpers.org/blog/2009/06/emersons-saadi.
20. Hammer Purgstall, *Geschichte der Schonen Persien Redekunste mit einer Bleuthenlese aus Zweyhundert Persischen Dichtern*, Vienna, 1818.
21. Browne, *From Firdawsi to Sa'di*.
22. Reynold A. Nicholson, *Translations of Eastern Poetry and Prose*, Cambridge: Cambridge University Press, 1922.
23. Arthur J. Arberry, *Immortal Rose*:

An Anthology of Persian Lyrics, London: Luzac, 1948.
24. Sir Lucas White King, *Tayyibat: The Odes of Sheikh Muslihu'd-din Sa'di Shirazi*, London: Luzac, 1926; and *Badayi: The Odes of Sheikh Muslihud-Din Sa'di Shirazi*, Berlin: Kavain, n.d. (c. 1925).
25. See Johan D. Yohannan, *The Poet Sa'di: A Persian Humanist*, Lanham MD: University Press of America and Bibliotheca Persica, 1987, p. 93.
26. See Forughi, *Kolliyat-e Sa'di*. See also his *Ghazaliyat-e Sa'di*.
27. See Katouzian, *Sa'di: The Poet of Life*, ch. 3.
28. See Hamidiyan, *Sa'di dar Ghazal*, ch. 2.
29. Ibid., p. 114.
30. Ibid., p. 102.
31. For a good summary of their views, see Yohannan, *The Poet Sa'di*, ch. 4.
32. Quoted in ibid. pp. 96–7.
33. See Nicholson's introduction to Lucas White King's *Badayi*, n.pag [2].
34. Forughi's *Kolliyat*, pp. 279–80.
35. See Katouzian, *Sa'di: The Poet of Life*, ch. 4. See further Homa Katouzian, 'Sufism in Sa'di, and Sa'di on Sufism', in Leonard Lewisohn, ed., *The Legacy of Medieval Persian Sufism*, London and New York: Khaneqahi Nimatullahi Publications, 1992.
36. *Kolliyat*, p. 566.
37. *Kolliyat*, p. 560.
38. *Kolliyat*, p. 442.
39. *Kolliyat*, p. 421
40. *Kolliyat*, p. 604.
41. *Kolliyat*, p. 617.
42. *Kolliyat*, p. 636.
43. *Kolliyat*, p. 419.
44. *Kolliyat*, p. 428.
45. *Kolliyat*, p. 417.
46. *Kolliyat*, p. 604.
47. *Kolliyat*, p. 418.
48. *Kolliyat*, p. 638.
49. *Kolliyat*, p. 603.
50. *Kolliyat*, p. 594.
51. *Kolliyat*, p. 458.
52. *Kolliyat*, p. 476.
53. *Kolliyat*, p. 458.
54. *Kolliyat*, p. 421.
55. *Kolliyat*, p. 525.
56. *Kolliyat*, p. 433.
57. *Kolliyat*, p. 524.
58. *Kolliyat*, p. 556.

POEMS

1. *Kolliyat*, pp. 560–61.
2. *Kolliyat*, p. 606.
3. *Kolliyat*, p. 560.
4. *Kolliyat*, pp. 559–60.
5. *Kolliyat*, p. 453.
6. *Kolliyat*, p. 438.
7. There are two puns here. The name Shirin, Farhad's beloved, means sweet. Being 'salty' in Persian is being humorous or teasing.
8. *Kolliyat*, p. 611.
9. *Kolliyat*, pp. 608–9
10. *Kolliyat*, p. 562.
11. *Kolliyat*, p. 481.
12. *Kolliyat*, p. 557.
13. *Kolliyat*, p. 521
14. *Kolliyat*, pp. 478–9
15. *Kolliyat*, p. 472.
16. *Kolliyat*, p. 452.
17. *Kolliyat*, p. 465.
18. *Kolliyat*, p. 451.
19. *Kolliyat*, p. 468.
20. *Kolliyat*, p. 494.
21. *Kolliyat*, p. 614.
22. *Kolliyat*, p. 618.
23. *Kolliyat*, p. 499.
24. *Kolliyat*, p. 637.
25. *Kolliyat*, p. 553.
26. *Kolliyat*, p. 573.
27. *Kolliyat*, p. 490.
28. *Kolliyat*, p. 454.
29. *Kolliyat*, p. 548
30. *Kolliyat*, p. 565
31. *Kolliyat*, p. 514
32. *Kolliyat*, p. 546.
33. *Kolliyat*, p. 457
34. *Kolliyat*, p. 463.
35. *Kolliyat*, p. 493.
36. *Kolliyat*, p. 564.
37. *Kolliyat*, p. 594
38. *Kolliyat*, p. 475.
39. *Kolliyat*, p. 637.
40. *Kolliyat*, pp. 464–5
41. *Kolliyat*, p. 463
42. *Kolliyat*, pp. 576–7.
43. *Kolliyat*, p. 552
44. *Kolliyat*, p. 257.

45. *Kolliyat*, pp. 469–70.
46. *Kolliyat*, pp. 568–9
47. The Persian word for 'sugar' is *shekar*, the name of Khosrow's mistress; *Shirin* means 'sweet' and was the name of Khosrow's favourite wife.
48. *Kolliyat*, p. 469.
49. *Kolliyat*, pp. 553–4
50. *Kolliyat*, p. 632.
51. *Kolliyat*, p. 504.
52. *Kolliyat*, p. 551.
53. *Kolliyat*, p. 625
54. *Kolliyat*, p. 505.
55. *Kolliyat*, p. 528
56. *Kolliyat*, p. 556.
57. *Kolliyat*, p. 549.
58. *Kolliyat*, p. 526.
59. *Kolliyat*, p. 604.
60. *Kollyiat*, p. 600
61. *Kolliyat*, p. 605.
62. *Kolliyat*, p. 488
63. *Kolliyat*, p. 546.
64. *Kolliyat*, pp. 433–4.
65. *Kolliyat*, p. 579
66. *Kolliyat*, pp. 428–9.
67. *Kolliyat*, pp. 466–7.
68. *Kolliyat*, p. 435.
69. *Kolliyat*, p. 575.
70. *Kolliyat*, p. 472.
71. *Kolliyat*, p. 432.
72. *Kolliyat*, pp. 578–9.
73. *Kolliyat*, p. 568.
74. *Kolliyat*, pp. 549–50.
75. *Kolliyat*, pp. 789–90.
76. *Kolliyat*, p. 789.
77. *Kolliyat*, pp. 787–8.
78. *Kolliyat*, pp. 796–7.
79. *Kolliyat*, pp. 787–8.
80. *Kolliyat*, p. 793.
81. *Kolliyat*, p. 785.

Index of first lines

Anyone passing by the lovers' lane 89

Beside your face others are pictures on the wall 67
By the dust under your feet I did not break my pledge 157

Careful is one who shuns the lovers' season 55
Come, it's time for peace, friendship and kindness 165

Does the cock not crow in time, tonight? 139
Do let me pass by your face 79
Do not believe, my love, that I have any other 59

Each time that wayward idol passes by me 103
Enough of taking off, I have no wings left 129
Ever since I set eyes on that beautiful face 65
Every day and night I almost decide 53

For you I feel something, something special 63

God, am I so fortunate that I see the beloved's face 123
God what a blessèd dawn was last night's union 137
Green is the valley where the beloved resides 163

He who has seen your face would know how I feel 81
He who lives without her 73
He would know how long is the night of separation 159

How soft is the garment on your figure 61

I am cheerful in this lush world of His 191
I am kept afar from my sweetheart 161
I am so bewitched by your look 87
I am so trapped in your love 179
If by your unkindness my heart is hurt 171
If I describe the pains of separation 169
If I die of your love in this world 51
If throwing an erotic look is sinful, I am immersed in sin 141
I have no patience to be without you 177
I know no-one who is not bewitched by you 117
In the breath that I die, for you I'll be longing 35
I said I'd get hard-hearted awhile 43
I still think of you even if you care not 77
I tried hard to hide the secret of desire 31
It's not just that no-one resembles you 93
It would be but a small loss 71
I've forgotten me since I've known her 47

Last night I felt the joy of life 131
Let me cry hard like the spring cloud 175
Let my body and soul be a sacrifice to you beloved 109
Let the people say I am drunk and in love 91
Little did I know that constancy and kindness you lack 151

Little fox, why did you not know your place 189
Love is not a story that can be written 119
Love with patience belongs to a heart of stone 41
Loving, after all, was not my invention 85

My luck is not a mirror at which you may look 69

Naught is more joyous than the beloved's word 167
None as enticing as you have I come across 115
No-one can come between us tonight 125
No pledge you ever made you did not break 153

One with an image of the cypress tree 107

Sleeping in an abode without the beloved 75
Stop being drunk all my life, I will not 33

That is not a face whose beauty I can express 99
The elixir of my life is in your mouth 173
The garden of beauty has not moulded a shoot like you 101
The human body is ennobled by the human soul 183
The most blissful night and auspicious day 145

The night of selfless lovers is too long 49
The pain of love is one which has no remedy 39
There is beauty, candlelight, wine and sweets this night 135
There is no life as royal as that of beggars 185
The sun does not deign to rise upon this night 149
The sweetness of her mouth is divine 113
The whole town belongs to the homeless person 187
Thinking of you at night my head was on fire 155
This one night in my beloved's embrace 127
Trees are in bloom, nightingales drunk 97

Whether or not my heart is patient in loving 83
Who am I, worthless me, to ask for your hand 37
Would anyone give up loving his sweetheart? 57

Years will pass on the dust of our dead rows 193
You, a part of paradise and sign of bliss 45
You have no pity for me at all 95
Your figure is beyond praise 111
You stepped into my life and I lost control 143
You went and I was a soulless face 133
You who deny the world of dervishes 195